Of *Water* *and* *Grief*

a memoir on life and death,
child loss and grief, and healing

Mandy Allender

ISBN: 979-8-218-75199-9

For my kids, who will
never have to hear me say I wish I had.

And my husband, without whom
I would never have survived it all.

chapter 1

My mother used to take us to the local community center in the morning. She would hand Adam, my oldest brother, a 20 dollar bill as we pulled up to the building. We would tumble out of the car, an excited stampede of arms and legs and shouts of "Bye, mom!" We had our bathing suits and towels in a bag, and a quarter for the pay-phone to call when we were ready to come home. Then she would then leave. She would just leave. My mother would blissfully drive away, just trusting that we would be fine, and she would see us, healthy, hale and whole, in a few hours time.

My brothers were so much bigger than me. Faster, smarter, stronger. Ryan, the middle brother, was around six years old, and sprinted away from the car as mom pulled out, not waiting for either of us. Adam, around seven, glanced back to make sure I was keeping up. "Come on, Mandy!" Shouted over his shoulder as we blazed through the front doors, and impatiently paid for admission; a few dollars each for the entire day. Admission covered the gymnasium, the cafeteria, the library, and the outside playground. There were hot tubs and kiddie pools and water slides, throngs of people and so much noise it made my head hurt. But we didn't care about any of that. All we cared about was the very center of the pool atrium; the main attraction; the object of all of our excitement and desire: the wave pool.

It was enormous. To my five-year-old eyes, it was the ocean. It started out shallow, and gradually got deeper and deeper until it was bottomless. Limitless. Unfathomable. It was terribly huge and terribly exciting. The smell of chlorine filled my nostrils as we ran onto the pool deck after hurriedly shoving our things into storage lockers. The waves were already running; giant mechanisms behind the walls at the deep end that pushed and pulled the water until it created waves taller than a person; waves that crashed and broke on the shallow shore.

Adam and Ryan, already strong swimmers, headed directly into the waves without a second thought. Despite not being able to swim, and not knowing that I didn't know how to swim, I ran right past the life jacket station and into the pool after them. I didn't know that they were supposed to watch out for me, and they had forgotten. I didn't know that I was supposed to stop and strap a jacket around my body. I didn't know there was danger, and I didn't care.

It was chilly, but I didn't notice. Excitement numbed the ache. As the water rose above my knees, the pressure of it held me back, and I was surprised how hard I had to push to continue moving forward, my eyes locked on my brothers. They were hooting and whooping, jumping into and over the waves just ahead of me. It looked so fun. I was going to do that too.

As I pushed deeper, the waves started lifting me off of the floor of the pool. Every other step no longer touched the ground, until my toes were just barely grazing the gritty surface. I felt my body lengthen as my tiptoes reached for the floor and I craned my neck trying to stretch tall enough, but I had no earthly idea how to keep myself above the water. I pressed on. After a few moments, I looked up and realized that the surface of the water was well above me. Confused, I thought, "How do I get up there?" I wasn't worried or afraid. I felt the pressure of wanting to breathe, that intense burning in my lungs, but no fear. There was no fear at all. I stopped trying to move, just frozen, staring up at the bright, faintly blue surface of the water, unimaginably far above my head. It was so beautiful. The way the water undulated, the light danced, and how quiet everything was. I was completely overcome with an incredible sense of peace, an inexorable calm in a moment that seemed to last for hours.

Without realizing I had closed them, I opened my eyes to find myself covered in blankets on a couch in the lifeguard station. There were several adults hovering over me, glancing at each other and then looking back at me. No sign of the peace from before, I was suddenly cold and scared. I had no idea what had happened, nor how I ended up on that couch, with those strangers. I had no idea that I had been rescued by a sharp-eyed lifeguard that saw me under the surface of the pool, not struggling nor trying to swim. I had no idea if someone did CPR, or whether or not I had stopped breathing when they finally pulled me out. I had no memory of any of that at all.

My brothers were completely unaware; they had never noticed that I was gone, nor had they witnessed the rescue of a little lifeless girl out of the pool. As soon as I fully came around, the lifeguards strapped a life-jacket onto my body, told me not to get in the pool without it, and turned me back out into the pool deck. I found my brothers as they were going down the water slides, and joined them in the fun. I never told them. I never told my parents. It would be many, many years before the memory came to me again.

I was born to be a mother.

That is a strong assertion to make, but believe me, it's not wrong. I was six years old when I found out that women had nipples to nurse their babies, and I realized that I wanted nothing more. I babysat my mom's friends' kids. I 'adopted' children on the playground at school. I laid in bed at night and imagined, over and over, the process of growing a human within my own body, and birthing that sweet, beautiful child, and then raising it. Bright, sparkly dreams full of sunshine and happiness. There was nothing I was more sure of than the fact that I was born to be a mother.

I grew up in a traditional household, in Edmonton, Alberta, Canada. We fit the typical North American profile: a working father, a stay at home mother, two older brothers, and me, the little sister. My parents had an incredibly connected and supportive relationship, and my mom loved being a mom. She was warm, and soft, and welcoming, and kind, and patient. She cooked all of our meals, kept the house, and loved us to distraction. I worshiped her. Her name was Nancy, and she was shortish, and roundish, and soft and gentle. She hugged with warm squinty eyes and kissed with a big ol' black mole just above the right side of her lip—if you drew a line from the edge of your nostril to the end of your mouth, it was at the halfway point. Mom colored her dark hair a soft caramel blonde so that she wouldn't look harsh like her mother did. She wore big, shiny, window-y glasses, and had a gap in her front teeth.

My father was her opposite in so many ways. Taller, and leaner, and sharper, and rougher. He was an acerbic intellect with a soft brown beard and a mischievous smile. His name was Gerald, but he went by Jerry, and he loved my mother deeply and well. Together they set the bar in my little heart for how all married couples should be.

My brothers were wild and beautiful, each of us only a year apart. I had no idea, growing up, how hard that was for my mother, but she made it seem easy. I adored my rough and tumble siblings, and they worshiped their tiny, stubborn, loud little sister. Even then, I was raw, tender, wide open; an exposed nerve, exquisitely sensitive. In my world, full of tears and aches, each day was a new opportunity for someone or something to hurt my feelings. Luckily, my family mostly delighted in their smallest, sweetest member, big feelings and all. I went out of my way to keep everyone happy, and everyone fell helpless to my every whim.

As a family, we spent weekends and vacations together; roadtrips to visit grandparents, baseball tournaments and assorted events. We never had lots of money, and camping was cheap and fun, and my parents were adventurous. My mom was a singer—an entertainer—and she always brought her guitar so we could sing around the campfire. She had the most beautiful voice I'd ever heard, then or since. Rich and deep, like molasses and warm butter, soothing and filled with love. My father was a master carpenter, and traveled all over Canada working on construction. We moved often, and I attended thirteen different schools from Kindergarten through graduation.

Even though we were what I now refer to as *a comfortable kind of poor*, my childhood was idyllic. I have always been grateful for the values my parents instilled in me, to be kind, to be smart, to be compassionate, and to work hard. They didn't set any limitations on me, but instead gave me the belief that I could do or be anything that I wanted to be. I mostly believed them.

One of the most formative parts of my childhood was my mother and father's powerful, all-encompassing love of reading. Our home exploded with books of all shapes and colors. Their passion for the written word spilled out onto me, and I began my life as a voracious reader. I was not a popular kid at any of the many schools I attended, and the librarians were always my best friends. Rather than be alone, I journeyed through the lives and adventures of innumerable wonderful characters. The Babysitters Club, and the Thoroughbred Series—I couldn't get enough of them. Garion and Belgarath, the Dragonriders of Pern, Wallie Smith and Sparhawk and Xanth; hundreds of characters in thousands of pages, each of them a steward to my growing imagination and burgeoning awareness of life and human nature. I read about Queen Porenn when I was nine years old – my first journey through the Belgariad – and she was described as *barren*; she was unable to have children. Immediately, my world was colored with the knowledge that it was possible to be infertile, and just as immediately, I worried. I began to imagine that the inside of my womb was a desert, cacti and all. 'What happens if,' I would ask my mom, over and over again, '… if I can't have any babies?'

Because, all I wanted to be was a mother. I dreamed of it. Yearned for it. Longed for it, deeply. I used to sit and look out my window every night and wish that the moon would make my baby dolls come to life. I hummed and swooned and crooned to pretend infants. For as long as I could remember, the pinnacle of my human existence was going to be the birth of my own child. The time I had to wait for my own babies was excruciating to me.

Years passed in that agony of childhood—time spent riding horses and learning how to learn, playing soccer and hours and hours outside—a miracle of being an under-parented, wildly free kid of the 80's. My family moved all around Alberta, and eventually ended up on Vancouver Island, just in time for Middle School.

By the time I was 12 years old, we had a computer and connection to the internet. The entire world opened up before me in new and exciting ways. It was around that time that I met Jonas playing a video game. I was pretending to be an adult in a role-playing adventure, and I was flattered that this adult was interested in me. We played more and more often together, until we were chatting every single day. Finally, after several months of spending time together online, I broke down and admitted to him that I wasn't a grown-up—I was just a young girl of not even thirteen. Much to my surprise and dismay, he admitted that he also wasn't a grownup! He was also pretending to get respect and be taken seriously in the online world, but he was only fourteen too!

I could hardly believe it. I didn't want to believe him. The real grownups in my life had talked about online predators, and I was pretty sure that this was what one looked and acted like. However, after a phone conversation and a few photographs in the mail, it turned out to be true. He was only 14, and lived in South Dakota, and together, Jonas and I began a long-distance relationship that lasted until he moved to Seattle for college. My family was living on Vancouver Island, and Seattle was near enough for me to drive down to see Jonas and his roommates, Brock and Alex, nearly every weekend.

That became our arrangement for the next two years; weekend trips, online romance, unending phone calls. I was *madly in love,* but our courtship was turbulent. When things were good, they were really, really good. Jonas was so smart and funny. He really seemed to admire and respect me. He told me I was beautiful. He said I was his best friend. We enjoyed spending time together, and we could talk for hours and hours.

When things were bad, though… they were awful. I was often confused—my relationship with Jonas didn't feel like the warm, comfortable love my parents shared, with rounded edges and gentle words. Ours felt like walking on sharp rocks, hot pavement, frosted glass. It felt wild and scary, with uncontrollable ups and downs. There were misunderstandings and disagreements. Shouting on the phone; explaining, mollifying, justifying, and just crying. Gentle proclamations of unending love, then jealous accusations. I could never tell which way was up.

My dad used to come in after I'd hung up the phone and tell me how much it hurt to hear the way Jonas made me feel. Mom would beg me to stand up for myself, to stop letting him treat me that way. Some part of me knew that our relationship wasn't healthy, but I just couldn't get clear. I couldn't figure it out. I loved him so much. I would do anything for him. I just wanted him to be happy. It all looked like love, and felt like love… sometimes.

Right before my 18th birthday, I graduated from high school. I had no plans nor pressing desire to go to college—there was no career goal or education in mind. I just wanted to have kids, and I couldn't get kids at university. Jonas and I had been in our long-distance relationship for several years already, and it was still hard. Exhausting. In a last ditch effort to make things work, I decided that the stress of the separation was what had made our relationship so turbulent, and that being together was the most obvious solution. So, despite the legal roadblocks, my parents' cautions, the uncomfortable realities of our relationship, and our extreme youth, Jonas and I flew to Hawaii and got married on the beach at sunset. I was nineteen years old, and my sweet little heart was full. Just like I'd always imagined, I was married, and we were going to have babies. All of my childhood dreams were quite rapidly coming true. The world was bright, life was good, and it wasn't even that hard.

chapter 2

J ust days after our wedding, Jonas and I moved to Sioux Falls, South Dakota to begin our grown-up lives. It was where his parents lived, and they were planning to help financially support us while we both attended school with plans to graduate, buy a house and then—BABIES. We had gone back and forth on this conversation over and over. I was very clear that I just wanted to have kids, but it was important to Jonas that we do things 'the right way,'—get an education, own a home, and be financially stable.

So, even though all I really wanted was just to be a stay-at-home mom, I picked a possible future career based on what would get me to my babies the soonest, and settled on Ultrasound Technologist—a sonographer. It was a two year program! I could be working and getting pregnant in two itty-bitty years. The only caveat to the program was that there was a distance portion: I had to do my clinical trials in a different city.

The first year and a half of our marriage was as turbulent as our courtship. For the first time, we were living together, and figuring out what it meant to be employees, adults, and spouses all at the same time. Oh, it was agony. There were moments, flashes of beauty when things were smooth and we were happy together; going to the movies or riding our bikes around the city. But when we fought? I couldn't figure out how to come up for air. Jonas was relentless. Somehow, every disagreement, every argument—even if I was the one that brought it up—left me in tears. Somehow, I was not doing it right. I didn't love him enough. I didn't try hard enough. I wasn't doing enough. Inevitably, every fight ended in my promises to try harder, to do better, to be more, all the while I was spinning internally, trying to figure out what had just happened.

We settled into a comfortable sort of routine where I went to school every day, and worked every evening at a local bank so we could pay our rent and have health insurance. Jonas enrolled in a business college while he and his buddy got a loan to start a video game company. We were both so busy that outside of fighting and occasional sex, it felt like we didn't see each other. Marriage was not really at all like I had imagined.

Time went by swiftly, and in January of our second year, it was time for me to leave Sioux Falls for the clinical portion of my degree. We decided that it made the most sense for Jonas to stay behind to run his company and complete his degree, while I traveled alone to Bentonville, Arkansas and moved into a tiny little one-room apartment for the seven month clinical period. I would finish my degree, and move home, and that was when life would finally begin. Just seven more months. It wasn't very long at all.

Less than two weeks into our brief separation, I received an email from my husband, which was strange enough—we didn't email, we called. There was an immediate clench of fear in my belly. It wasn't typical. It was weird.

I sat in front of my monitor, and opened the email, and felt the lifeforce drain out of me as I read his words. My body began to collapse beneath me. It was my worst possible fear.

> "I feel like I gave up a lot of once-in-a-lifetime opportunities to be with you, like dating other girls and all of the things I sacrificed to make our long distance relationship work."

My eyes skipped forward to the end in panic. I could hardly breathe. *What is the point? What is he saying here??*

"I don't know where to go from here. I know that no matter how I angle this, or bring it up, you will get upset and stop listening to what I'm saying and thinking about it, and just be emotional. I don't blame you for being emotional, but I want you to actually think about what I'm saying."

Don't be emotional? '*Actually think*?' My entire brain turned offline at the first sentence. *You gave up a lot? Dating other girls? What about me? What about leaving my home, my country, my family? Dating other girls???*

I slowed my breathing and forced my eyes to focus on the meat of the email. I carefully read the rest, and digested the message. He didn't want to be married anymore… he also didn't want a divorce. He just didn't know what he wanted, but he was pretty sure it wasn't me.

The shock that rang through my body was unlike anything I had ever felt before. The tears came, and welled up out of me uncontrollably. I lost my breath. I curled up in a ball, feeling like I had actually been viscerally punched. I cried, and cried, and cried. Even though our marriage was not wonderful, I still did not believe that I would be left, abandoned, devastated in that way. I loved him. I loved him so much. I was willing to do any-thing—absolutely anything—to change his mind and make him stay and yet he was leaving. *He was leaving me.* The ache in my chest and the lump in my throat were choking me. I struggled to breathe. I was drowning in sorrow. I was losing everything. Not just my marriage, nor my husband, but the entire future that was so bright and shiny-beautiful in my mind. I was losing the children I didn't even have yet.

I was worthless.

I fought for my marriage for weeks and weeks. I sent desperate pleas to Jonas, begging him to reconsider. I asked him to tell me what I had done wrong. I implored him for a list of what to fix so that I could make things work. We spent hours and hours on the phone. He was cold, and distant, and had neither compassion nor empathy for me or the position he had put me in.

I was alone.

Barely two weeks into a brand new city, with no connections and no friends, I was alone and devastated and forlorn. Not only was I miles and miles away from my family, but I was in a strange place. I couldn't get away from my sorrow. In desperation, I joined a dance studio and started taking ballet classes. I started going out for drinks in the evenings with some of my coworkers. I found a library and signed out rank after rank of my ever present, steadfast companions—books—and even that wasn't enough. The ache inside of me, the hole was so deep it could not be filled. In a last ditch attempt to find more connection, to feel less alone, I emailed everyone that I could think of. My entire contact list. One at a time, all of my old friends and acquaintances, looking for some way to keep my head above the surface as I navigated the murky waters of painful, aching isolation in my early twenties. I started text messaging everyone I had a number for—for the right reasons, and the wrong reasons. I just couldn't stand being alone with myself.

In March, after months of push and pull, tug-of-war conversing and trying to stay married, I convinced Jonas to come with me to a concert. I had bought the tickets months before, and we both loved the band. "It doesn't mean anything," I told him. "We don't have to decide anything. Let's just enjoy the concert. That's all we have to do."

We drove separately, and met at the concert venue. The night was incredible. Magical. A once in a lifetime experience. My all-time favorite band, Great Big Sea, was playing in the US, and I had gotten tickets, AND it was the anniversary of their first concert. I knew the words to every song, and Jonas swayed beside me, looking content and pleased to be there. My eyes filled with tears as the band came out for the encore, and sang the most beautiful *a capella* rendition of Old Brown's Daughter. They streamed down my face openly as the entire theater erupted in cheers and hoots and whistles. My heart was absolutely full. Contentment, joy, excitement. I looked over and smiled at Jonas, and he grinned back at me. A thrill of hope ran up my spine. It felt okay. Maybe things were going to be okay.

At the end of the concert, we held hands as we walked out to his car together. We decided to pick up my car the next morning. I was a bundle of nerves on the drive back to what used to be our home, but excited nerves. Hopeful nerves. We were going to be okay.

I walked into the apartment that no longer felt like mine, noticing a slight shake to my hands. It had been months of solitude and self-loathing; I was just so ready to feel love again. It was as though Jonas felt exactly the same way, and we didn't hesitate or pause—we walked directly into the bedroom. I sat down on the bed, *our bed*, and Jonas sat beside me. He smelled like him. Like my husband. My best friend. He smelled like we were going to be okay. He didn't make eye contact with me, but brushed a lock of my hair behind my ear. My heart started pounding uncontrollably as he leaned towards me, and I knew he wanted to kiss me. I leaned away, and ducked down to catch his eye with my own and sat up straight as I said softly, "I love you."

He paused, and his hand dropped away from my face.

I leaned closer towards him, and said again, a little louder, "Jonas. I love you."

Jonas looked away from me, and my eyes immediately filled with tears. The rejection was a second kick in the stomach. He was willing to kiss me, and willing, I think, even to have sex with me, but he was not willing to say that he loved me. He did not love me.

I stood up wordlessly, and walked out of the apartment, and got a ride back to my car. I drove back to Arkansas that night, alone and devastated all over again. It was the longest night of my life, driving home in the dark utterly isolated on the long, black highway. All I could see through tear-blurred vision were my two headlights on the pavement. It felt like a perfect example of my life: alone in the dark dark, no one around, and nothing to be seen outside of the tiny circle directly in front of me.

The next morning, I awoke to a text message from a friend of Jonas's.

'I'm so sorry, Mandy. I can't let him keep hurting you like this. Jonas has been cheating on you. He has someone else. It's been going on since October.'

While I had wondered if it were ever possible, I continually convinced myself that it couldn't be so. I believed him when he told me there was no one else. I ignored my guts and my intuition, and let him assure me that the problem was *not* another girl. And in a single moment, all of my hopes and dreams of fixing my marriage and going on to have the life that I had imagined shattered into a thousand, million painful pieces, each one slicing into me.

I immediately called and confronted Jonas with the truth that I had been given, and he did not deny it. In what was one of the most powerful, pivotal moments of my life, I told him the choice was no longer his: it was over. I wanted a divorce, and I never wanted to see or hear from him again, ever. I hung up the phone, and took off my wedding ring, and threw it across my empty apartment.

And then I screamed.

I broke down in tears and collapsed. The pain was unimaginable. It was physical, palpable. It hurt like a car wreck. It hurt like I had been crushed. I couldn't catch my breath. I cried so hard my nose started bleeding. Laying on the floor, with blood on my face and smeared along the backs of my hands, I started to calm down. I started to breathe again. And then I started casting about for something *else*.

I can't be here, I thought to myself. *I can't stay here. I can't do this. I need out.*

I wanted an escape. I needed someone to rescue me. I picked up my phone and called my mother—I definitely wanted, needed my mom.

'Hello?' My dad's voice rang out of my mother's cell phone, and I was immediately disappointed. I tried to hide the tears in my voice, but I was a mess.

'Is mom there?'

'She's not, Mand. She's not home. What's going on? Are you okay?' Dad's voice was deeply concerned.

I wasn't okay, and I didn't want to talk to him. I just wanted mom. He wouldn't get it. He wouldn't understand. He probably wouldn't even care. He was just... dad.

"Mandy? What happened?"

Despite my reluctance to share with *not my mom*, the words came spilling out of my mouth before I could stop them.

"Jonas was cheating on me, dad. He left me. It's over." The tears started back up again as I poured out. "I hate this. I can't do this anymore. I want to come home, Dad. Can I come home? Please let me come home."

I let the phone fall away from my face as I sobbed and sobbed. Jonas left me, I was alone and worthless, and my mom wasn't even there to help.

"Mand. Mandy..." I heard my dad's voice, thin and tinny coming out of the speaker that was on the bed. I picked up the receiver and held it to my ear and held my breath. He must have heard the crying finally slow, as he began, "I'm so sorry, Mand. I'm so sorry. I know how much this hurts. Of course your mother and I want you to come home."

I braced myself. He wasn't going to say the right thing. Dads never did.

He continued, "We *always* want you to come home if you want to come home, babe. But if you leave now..." he paused, "If you leave now, he's left you with nothing. You come home and you have nothing."

I didn't say anything. I just sat there and absorbed what he was telling me.

You have nothing.

"But Mand," he went on, "If you can push through... if you

can stay for just a few more months, and finish?" I could hear the heart in his voice, the love in his words. "...if you finish—then you have a degree, a career, and a job that no one can ever, ever take from you. Not even Jonas can take that away from you."

I let my held breath blow out explosively. What he was saying made so much sense, and I hadn't considered it. I sniffled.

"You can always come home if you need to. But if you can push through, if you can stay... you'll never regret it. You'll never be sorry.'

I nodded at the phone as the gravity of what he was saying sunk in. He was right. I needed to stay and finish the program and get my degree. I had already lost everything else—I didn't need to lose all of my hard work, too.

A small smile came to my lips as I told dad that I was so glad he answered the phone. I wanted my mom, but I was so sure she would have just told me to pack my bags and come home. That was what I *wanted*. What I needed was dad's love—and dad's logic. He said exactly the right thing.

And so it was decided. I was going to go home, back to Canada where I was loved and supported and needed... I was just going to finish my ultrasound degree first.

chapter 3

All of the reaching out I had done those first weeks in Arkansas meant that I had an impressive bank of people that I was corresponding with; some daily, some weekly, some just occasionally. Friends from high school, old internet buddies—people that responded, and people that fell away after a few letters… oh, and also, Jonas's old Seattle roommate, Brock.

It had been a few years since I had last seen him, but I remembered Brock as a tall, kind, charismatic fellow with a lovely smile and an intensity that made you feel like the most important person in the world. He also had really nice feet.

I didn't reach specifically out to him, and I have no idea why he chose to respond, but we emailed each other daily during those long, lonely months. He heard my piercing sorrow, and didn't try to take it away from me. He shared with me the minutiae of his daily life, his problems and his foibles. It felt so normal. Long, rambling emails with nothing of consequence. Like we were correspondents in the late 1800's. Like we could just be people together. Like he didn't have to fix me, and I didn't have to protect myself. Like I wasn't broken.

It only made sense, then, that when Brock's family invited me to the wedding they were hosting at another small town in Arkansas, only a few hours from me—well, of course I had to go.

The days leading up to the wedding, I wondered if I was making a poor decision. I was still heartbroken over the loss of my marriage, and had lost my faith and trust in men. Pretty much all of them.

I wasn't interested in any kind of new relationship, and anyway, Brock was dating a girl named Ava. Beyond that, I just wasn't very good company.

I hemmed and hawed, back and forth, over and over, trying to decide if I should go to the wedding or if I should just stay home. *I don't really have the money,* I told myself, *and I don't really have the time.* The wedding was in July, just two weeks before my graduation from Ultrasound school, and my final projects were waiting for me.

Nevertheless, on the afternoon of the rehearsal dinner, there was no maybe—I got permission to leave work a few hours early, grabbed an overnight bag, got in my navy green Jeep Wrangler and... drove. It was as though the choice had already been made for me. The compulsion was irresistible, and I was halfway there before I realized what I was doing.

I felt a momentary thrill of icy fear, and decided that it was time to make myself some promises. No matter what happened, at the wedding or in the future, there were things that mattered too much to ignore. And so, loudly and foolishly, on the way to the wedding, hand over my heart and witnessed by the sun, I swore my own vows to myself.

I promise I will never let someone hurt me like Jonas hurt me again.

I promise I will never be too weak to leave.

I promise I will remember how strong I am.

I promise, promise, promise to always put myself first.

Somehow, those promises helped.

When I pulled into the parking lot of the restaurant, late, I was suddenly sure I had made an error. There was no reason for me to be at that wedding. I hadn't seen Brock in years. Sure, I was invited, but I was a stranger.

What the heck am I doing here?

I felt the beginnings of panic in my chest.

This is absolutely a mistake.

I gripped the steering wheel until my knuckles turned white, and then took a few deep breaths.

It's okay, Mandy, I tried to rationalize, *You are allowed to be here.*

My heart rate started to slow, and I was able to blink my eyes open and look around. "Besides," I said out loud to myself, "You deserve to spend some time with kind people who care about you." I nodded. Really, I was just there for friendship and fellowship. There was no reason at all to think about how sweet Brock was. Or how handsome he was. Or funny. Or how magnificent the memory of his smile still made me feel. No reason to think about that *at all.*

As I finally climbed out of my car, the gravel in the parking lot grumbled under my feet; every step, each crunch a resounding, "WRONG. WRONG. WRONG." I stared at my shoes and felt my hands shake with nerves as I paced stiffly towards the entrance, when I realized I heard another crunch of gravel coming towards me.

"Right. Right. Right."

I looked up towards the noise, and saw a brilliant grin, shining eyes, and a whole lot of lanky Southern confidence wrapped in a smashing salmon-colored button-down. My knees went suddenly weak, and I froze. Brock chirruped out a friendly, "Hello," closed the distance between us, and wrapped me in a hug that warmed me to my soul. As we pulled apart, I looked way, way up at him and blurted, "You're so much taller than I remember!"

And he was. Taller, and handsome-er. He was… just so much more than I remembered. He smiled and asked about my drive as he guided me towards the dinner, and all of my trepidations melted away.

I was safe.

I glanced around the table and noticed almost immediately that Brock's on-again off-again girlfriend Ava wasn't there, and felt a stab of impropriety. I had just been devastated by a disloyal partner, and I wasn't about to walk any portion of that same path.

I caught Brock's eye and leaned over and whispered, "Where's Ava?"

"We had a fight yesterday," he told me, "and she decided not to come." He shrugged. "I don't think it's going to work out. I probably just need to break up with her." And just like that, we moved on. We chatted as though we had always been friends. It was easy. Comfortable. Right. Despite feeling unsettled about the whole situation with Ava, I squared my shoulders and decided to just enjoy the weekend for what it was—a short time with lovely people who were happy to have me there. I didn't need to manufacture something to worry about.

As the rehearsal dinner wound down, members of the wedding party drifted away to their hotel rooms. I was unsure of the next 'right thing' to do; Brock had told me that there was an extra bed in the hotel room he was sharing with his brother, but suddenly his girlfriend's absence was almost a presence. I walked alone back to my car to get my overnight bag and decided to just drive home instead. It seemed wise. The dinner was enough. I wanted to avoid doing what *felt* right, but instead do what *was* actually right. Instead of grabbing my bag, I turned on my heel to walk back to Brock, and let him know that I wasn't staying.

On my way to tell Brock my decision, I bumped into Brock's mother Judy; a petite woman with a powerful pixie cut and an even more powerful personality. She was thrumming with the excitement of one of her three sons getting married, and had enjoyed several glasses of wine at dinner. I will never be sure if it was the wine or just her brazen way that prompted her to grab me by the elbow and say, "We really like you, Mandy. You fit right in with us." Then, she threw her arm around my shoulder as she escorted me to the door of Brock's room. She turned the knob, pushed the door open, and leaned over and said quietly into my ear, "It's totally okay with me if you have sex with my son tonight,"

My eyes bulged and I gasped in surprise. I was spluttering out an awkward, "Um…" as Brock pulled the door the rest of the way open and welcomed me in. I stared in startled confusion as Judy hugged Brock and said goodnight, oblivious or uncaring as to the internal chaos she had just created within me. I had no idea how to process or even move forward from that moment. I was completely stunned.

Brady, the youngest Allender brother, broke the ice by shouting, "Hello!" and pointing to the bed that was meant to be his. "You'll sleep there," he announced as he settled down under some blankets on the couch. He was already wrapped up and ready for bed, and fell promptly asleep, as only a seventeen year old can.

Despite my initial misgivings, I ended up staying and Brock and I remained awake, on separate beds, talking until almost 4am. We were utterly captivated by each other. At some point, I gave him a breakdown of a long list of young men that I had considered friends who all eventually ended up confessing that they were romantically interested in me. I jokingly warned him that I was just a really nice person, and people tended to fall in love with me even though I wasn't interested. I cautioned him to be on his guard. He assured me that I had nothing to fear—it wouldn't happen. He promised me that there was absolutely no way he was going to fall in love with me.

The following morning, Brock, Brady and I got up and ready for the full day of "wedding activities." Family breakfast, military museum, lunch at a special restaurant, and then finally the wedding ceremony and reception. I didn't really know anyone there besides Brock, and he was a main contender in all of the events, so I occupied myself for the day by taking as many pictures as possible. Mostly everything we did was a blur. I was watching all of his interactions, and feeling all of the sensations within my body, and wavering back and forth between being pretty sure that Brock was into me, while also staunchly convincing myself that it *wasn't possible*. I wasn't supposed to be into him either. I was still far too angry at Jonas, and also still distrusting of men in general. There was no reason for us to be into each other.

I didn't see Brock at all during the actual wedding; I sat alone at the back of the cute little chapel. But as soon as the ceremony was over, he sought me out and we drove over to the reception in my Jeep together. We talked the whole time. When he asked me to dance, I felt like I was dreaming.

We are just friends, I told myself.

It doesn't mean anything.
He's just being nice.

We slow-danced under twinkle lights. Our hands were clasped out in front of us, and the weight of his other hand on my lower back took my breath away. I leaned my head forward just a little, his manly smell filling my chest, and he rested his cheek on my hair. I could have sworn I felt him sigh. In that moment, I wanted so badly to forget everything that I had promised myself, everything I had sworn; just forget all of the distrust and disdain I had for men. I wanted to ignore all of it, and I desperately wanted Brock to want me too.

Instead, I reminded myself that, in just two short weeks, I would be finished with ultrasound school. I was planning to pack up all of my things and drive my Jeep home to Canada. Even if I felt something for him, it was pointless. I wasn't staying. He knew I was going home, *and* he promised that he wasn't going to fall in love with me.

I sighed. There wasn't really any reality in which a relationship between us happened. Besides, he still had Ava. Even though he said he was going to break up with her, he hadn't yet. I had no proof that he would, no reason to trust him. Regardless of what the butterflies in my stomach were telling me, I sternly told myself to just enjoy the dance, and then move on. Move home.

As the reception wound down, we realized it was getting late, so Brock and I mentioned that we were going to head back to the hotel. Brady jumped up and announced, "Oh yeah! I'll come too!"

Brock drove my jeep, and I sat in the passenger seat. The Fray was playing loudly through the stereo, and the windows were down. My hair whipped all around, and I idly chatted with Brady, sitting in the back but leaning forward between us.

'I never knew, I never knew that everything was falling through, that everyone I knew was waiting on a cue...'

My cheeks ached from smiling so hard. My heart was pounding. Maybe it was the drink I had had at the reception, or maybe it was just a reckless thrill. All I could hear was my own voice in my head, saying over and over, *Just take his hand, Mandy. Just do it.*

He likes you. Take his hand. Just do it.

I closed my eyes and took a deep breath to summon the courage to put my hand on his…

'Everyone knows I'm in over my head, over my head, eight seconds left in overtime, she's on your mind…'

… and felt his hand take mine instead.

I swear, my heart exploded in my chest. It was electric. We didn't talk, we didn't even make eye contact, we just sat there in the car for the rest of the drive, holding hands and feeling our feelings and smiling like fools.

Even Brady had nothing else to say.

When we got back to the bed and breakfast, we found that most of Brock's close family had already left the reception as well. There was a large group of people in the hot tub, so we joined them. Brock and I sat next to each other and participated in the conversation, each holding a beer in the hand that wasn't under the water. We felt like we were so clever. Secretly holding hands. Under the water.

Eventually it got late enough that the entire wedding party retired to their rooms, including Brock, Brady and I. Only, we weren't tired. We were so high on each other that we decided to watch a show until we got sleepy. Brady sat down on the couch and put on an episode of "Arrested Development"—I'd never seen it before, but it made Brock laugh his big, beautiful laugh, so I immediately loved it.

Brock and I were sitting on the floor, leaning on the couch, and we held hands under the blanket. Secretly. We watched an episode or two, happy to be next to each other and smiling at one another occasionally until Brock unexpectedly leaned over and kissed me very gently on my temple.

I melted. Absolutely. From the inside out. You know that feeling… the one that starts in the bottom of your gut and spreads outward? Pure joy. I couldn't believe it. Gosh, I just couldn't believe that this sweet, kind, beautiful giant was attracted to me. Little me. Worthless me. Unwanted me. I lost my mind a little as he paused with his lips on my brow a second and breathed in my smell. My eyes closed and I was in ultimate bliss.

Brady must have noticed the kiss too, because he jumped off the couch as if he'd been slapped. Without saying a word, he darted across the room, shot out through the door and let it slam shut behind him. Brock and I looked at each other and laughed. We had no idea what had just happened, where he had gone, or when he was going to return.

We spent that whole night getting to know each other better. I know, I know... you think that's some euphemism for gettin' down... but it's not. To this day, I don't know that anyone believes us. We just talked. We held hands and talked and asked questions and told stories and laughed. Oh, how we laughed. I knew I was going back to Canada. Brock knew that he had to talk to Ava—he didn't want to move forward with me in any way without being totally open and honest with her; without ending their relationship officially. Since my marriage had just ended in infidelity, we both agreed that it mattered. It mattered so much.

Besides, we just kept waiting for Brady to come back.

We fell asleep—face to face, fully clothed, and holding hands—in the same bed around 4am.

The morning came and went, and we rolled up to 'breakfast' at nearly ten o'clock. We walked in together to a room-full of knowing looks, elbows, and grinning nods. It appeared that we were the butt of the joke of the dining room, but we didn't even care. We only had eyes for each other.

As soon as brunch was over, the rest of Brock's family packed into their vehicles and started the trek back to their respective homes. Brock and Brady had driven to Arkansas together and there was no choice. They couldn't stay. Their drive was over fifteen hours, and Brock had to work the next morning. But none of us were ready to let go yet. When Brock asked if I wanted to go see a movie with him, of course I said yes.

Brady came with us, and we went to The Pirates of the Caribbean. I'm sure the movie was great, but I hardly remember any of it.

I was sitting next to Brock. Those words kept shouting through my mind. "This is BROCK. I'm sitting next to BROCK. I'm holding hands with BROCK," over and over again, trying simultaneously to wake, yet not to wake from what seemed like a beautiful, impossible dream.

The movie ended, and we tried to part ways again. Again, it just wasn't time. We couldn't make it time. Not yet. Brock kept looking to Brady for something: Permission? Support? Acknowledgement? Brady had the biggest grin on his face. You could tell from the first instant that he was all in, the world's best wingman, and he suggested that we all go out for lunch.

I knew we were just stalling, taking up as much time with each other as we possibly could. Leaving was going to be painful. Suddenly I wasn't so sure about what I wanted, or that I should be going back to Canada, or that all men were complete trash. I wasn't sure about anything at all. I didn't know what to do. As we sat at the table, eating lunch, we talked about what the next few weeks could look like. We promised to keep in touch, although not with any formal understanding of what that meant.

All we seemed to agree on was: "We'll figure something out."

And then, finally, it was time. There were no more minutes to waste, no more excuses to make. There was no other choice but to say goodbye. Brock walked me to the driver's seat of my Jeep, and opened the door for me. I turned towards him, and he touched his forehead to mine as he held my hands in his. I breathed in deeply, pulling in his smell, as fully as I could, and held my breath—I wanted to keep a little bit of him with me. He looked into my eyes, forehead to forehead, and whispered, "Hey Mand… I'm *so in like* with you," Then he slowly, softly, gently kissed my lips. An electric shock went through my entire body.

It felt like a first kiss.

I paused, eyes closed and body frozen in a moment that I wanted never, ever to end. Then I exhaled, let go of his hands and my breath, and got into my car. He shut the door for me, and I waved out the window with my eyes full of tears as I drove away.

I kept glancing back at him in the rearview mirror for as long as I could, as the sun shone, and the light sparkled, and he stood with his hands in his pockets and watched me go.

I was absolutely elated and utterly empty in the very same moment.

chapter 4

Brock immediately began an unceasing campaign to see me again. Even though I had two weeks of my ultrasound program left, he bought plane tickets for me to fly to Charlotte the day after school ended. And somehow the only tickets he was able to get had me staying for a month.

He is so in like with me.

Brock also told me that he went to Ava's house as soon as he arrived back in town, and told her it was over. For real over, not just on a break over. He didn't give me the dirty details, but he told me she was upset, and that she blamed it on me. I carried a heavy bit of guilt—even though I'd tried so hard to do the right thing, we had still hurt her.

The two weeks of wrapping up school flew by in a blur, and the next thing I knew, I was sitting on an airplane as it was landing in Charlotte, North Carolina, and I again wondered what the heck I was doing. Surely, it wasn't as magical as I remembered. Surely, he wasn't as sweet and special and wonderful as I thought. Surely, I was just lonely and trapped in make-believe.

The plane landed and I walked towards the baggage claim, my heart in my throat again as I second-guessed all of my life decisions up until that point.

Will he still like me? Will I still like him? Will the kissing be wonderful?

Oh my gosh… will he want to have sex??

Thought and worry fell away as my eyes found his, striding

towards me with purpose and desire. He scooped me up into a hug, spun me around in a joyful arc, pressed his lips into mine, and everything was right.

I flew to Charlotte for a month, and then I just stayed. Brock didn't want me to leave, and I didn't want to go either. We were so good together. So smooth, so comfortable, so sweet. I flew back to Arkansas, got into my Jeep and instead of driving to Canada, I drove back to Brock. However, despite how easy it all felt, I stayed anxious about jumping into a new relationship so soon after being kicked out of my old one. I didn't want to move too fast, nor get too comfortable. I stayed on guard. I didn't allow myself to completely trust any of the things that Brock said to me with love in his eyes. I had just learned the hard way that boys can say lots of lovely things without ever meaning any of it. And after all, I had promised myself.

Weeks went by, though, and my life stayed dreamy-beautiful. Full of so much light and joy and glittery sunshine. Brock was my perfect man, a knight in shining armor. We had somehow found each other out of the darkness of my great loss, and we were happy. We ran errands together. We watched shows together. We got stuck in bed all day together, talking, laughing, enjoying, exploring. We talked about future children—Brock wanted kids too; just not quite yet. He wasn't ready, and that was okay.

Before I knew it, it was late July, and we swayed together on the back patio of his beautiful townhome, under the moon and stars, arms wrapped around each other, his cheek resting on my head. He sang to me as he cooked me dinner, loud and off key, and I watched him with a sparkle in my eyes. He took me up to his parent's lake house, and brought home fresh flowers from work. It was all so perfect.

We were just so in love.

Slowly, my tender heart opened to the possibility that this could be the real thing, and I really was safe. Brock loved me in a way that made me feel like being myself was okay. He let me love him in a way that made me feel whole. As long as we were together, we were bathed in the sweet, summery glow of sunset.

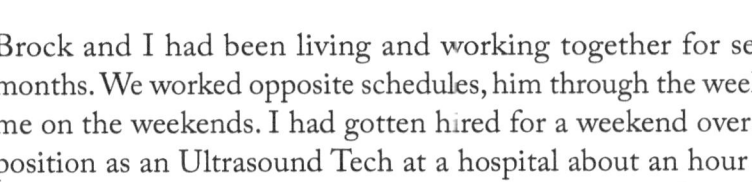

Brock and I had been living and working together for several months. We worked opposite schedules, him through the week and me on the weekends. I had gotten hired for a weekend overnight position as an Ultrasound Tech at a hospital about an hour away from our home, so most days, Brock was at work while I was home by myself, filling my time and trying to find things to do.

The first time I sat at his computer and found Pornography, it caught me by surprise, but it wasn't a huge deal. I knew it was a normal thing that guys did. It most certainly wasn't my first exposure to porn. When I brought it up that evening, I was completely honest with him: I wasn't cool with it while we were together; it made me uncomfortable and I wanted him to stop. It was hard for me to ask him to change for me, to set that boundary, but I made it clear that I wasn't willing to stay in a relationship with someone who watched porn while we were together. We had something really special, and I wanted to hold on to it. Brock was charmingly reassuring. Of course he would stop, he didn't know it would bother me, no problem at all.

The second time I found pornography, several weeks later, I was so confused. Had he not heard me? Was I not clear enough the first time? Really, it had just been a few weeks—it seemed impossible that he would have forgotten. I hesitated to bring it up again. I didn't want to be a bother, a nag—I didn't want to somehow push him away. I really wanted him to remain in love with me, and my fears immediately skewed into abandonment again. If I told him how the porn made me feel, he would definitely maybe leave me. Things were just so good... my life was so good. My heart was so cared for. The sex was so amazing. I didn't want to mess it up. I started to wonder if it would be possible for me to continue on without mentioning it, and just hope for the best.

But... I had promised myself.

Despite my hesitation to ruin things, I brought it up again, as openly and honestly as I could. I told him how upset it made me that he didn't listen to me the first time. I told him that I found it equal to infidelity, and I couldn't handle being cheated on, even just with porn. I told him that, if he wasn't willing to stop watching porn, he needed to tell me immediately, so I could just leave. I was direct, and clear, and my delivery could leave absolutely no doubt: if it happened again, we were over.

Brock listened kindly, patiently and then sweetly chuckled and hugged me when I was through. His smiling eyes and gentle kisses immediately calmed my fears. He told me that he didn't realize that I was serious about all that; none of his other girlfriends minded when he'd watched porn. It was kind of a gift to me, he said. To give me a break, he said. But, as he finally fully understood the depth of my concern, he would never do it again. Promise. Pinky-swear. Hope to die.

I was SO relieved. I just knew that he had heard me, and he definitely understood that I wasn't going to be a fool, and stay and continue being hurt. The father of my children wasn't going to watch Porn. I'd already learned that lesson. I was stronger than that. I didn't need a man, and I didn't have any problem leaving. Instead, I was so proud that we'd been strong enough to talk about pornography and our true feelings, to be honest with each other, and to deal with hard things together. I was delighted. We had overcome.

Until the next time.

The next time, the third time, I broke down. It had been months and I felt like we were truly past it. I had stopped worrying. I finally didn't feel a clench of fear in my chest every time I sat down at the computer, the niggling worry that said, 'what if?'

And yet, there it was. Plain as day, not even hidden from me. Porn. Again.

I cried and cried. My perfect man. My hero. My knight. Everything fell dark inside of me as my sobs shook my body, and I grieved the loss of the relationship I thought I had. My soulmate. My best friend. My forever.

He was a fraud. A scoundrel. A charlatan.

I was so ashamed, and so shaken. I could hardly move. The ache in my chest was so huge. The betrayal felt bigger than when I had found out about Jonas's other woman. My tears were endless. I loved him so much, and I wanted forever so badly. It hurt to know that I would never have his arms around me again. It hurt to know that I would never kiss his big, soft lips again. It hurt to know that I would never make him smile again. But I had made an ultimatum, and my resolve required action. I had sworn vows. I packed my bags and set them by the door. I was honest. I did not bluff. The porn had returned and I was leaving.

I promise I will never stay and be hurt again.

I cried all through the rest of that day. I cried as I sat on the floor of the shower and poured myself out. I cried as he walked through the door and concernedly asked me what was wrong as he tried to hug me. I cried when I pushed him away and told him that I'd found porn again. I cried as I yelled that he clearly didn't hear me or believe me. I cried when I told him that he betrayed me. I cried when I told him that I was leaving.

And then… I laughed.

I laughed when he told me he really didn't know that it mattered to me that much—because he did. I laughed when he said that he wouldn't do it again—because he had. I laughed when he told me that he would stop—because he wouldn't. Fool me once.

And then Brock cried. Tears poured down his face as he begged me not to leave, said that he would get help, promised that it would get better. He said that he didn't want to lose me, couldn't lose me. He said that we would fix this together, and he couldn't do it without me. He needed me.

I looked fully into the beautiful face of the man that I loved, and knew that I didn't want to go… but more than that, I didn't want to stay. I told him that I was sorry, but I was leaving.

And I left.

I got in my car and drove. I had no idea where to go. I pulled into the gas station less than a mile from our home, shifted the car to park, and I called my mom. We didn't really speak all that often; mom's life was busy and mine was just getting started. She had come to accept that I only called when I was upset, or hurt, or needed something, and she was okay with it. She knew that, if she didn't hear from me, it was because I was doing well.

Mom picked up the phone, and said, 'Hello?'

The words tumbled from my mouth without preamble.

"Mom. I think Brock's addicted to pornography."

She waited patiently as sobs poured out anew, the pain of bringing something hard to light. She was just so easy to talk to, even the hard things. Mom never tried to fix or instruct or correct. She didn't get angry or outraged on my behalf. She just listened.

"Oh, Mand..."

Her silence wasn't oppressive, it was comforting. I mumbled through tears and hiccups about how the first time, I explained that I wouldn't tolerate it, and then I had found more, and that basically my life was ruined forever.

"I'm so sorry, babe," she whispered gently. "I don't understand why it happens. I don't get it at all. I know that I would feel the exact same way if that happened to me."

I sniffled, and wiped wetness away from my red, achy eyes. I had been crying all day, and I was just so tired.

"I don't know what to do, mom," I moaned, " I don't want to stay with him if he can't stop watching porn. It feels so awful. It just… it just feels like he's cheating on me. And I think I should leave."

"I know what you mean, Mand. And I can't tell you what to do," Mom paused, and it was quiet for a beat. And then two. "But I can tell you what I did when your dad had an affair."

Shock.

My entire body froze. I couldn't even blink. My vision zoomed out and my breath caught. Affair? Dad had an affair? MY dad? Jerry?? It couldn't be true. My parents were in love. Deep, respectful, abiding love. They were the prime example, the alpha and omega of marriage. *My dad cheated on my mom?*

I had absolutely no idea.

Mom went on to tell me, through the fog of time and half-forgotten memories, about dad's affair, the other woman, how she found out, and how she'd responded—the Christmas she kicked him out, the hours of silent tears so her children wouldn't know, and his phone call begging her to let him come home.

Suddenly, I remembered. All of it.

My heart swelled with empathy and pain as I remembered walking into my mother's bedroom in the middle of the night and finding her crying on the floor. I didn't know then, sweet little me, how broken my mother had felt. I didn't know what it meant for her to wipe away the tears, and cuddle me up into her arms and tell me that she was okay. I didn't know what it cost her to carry on, and carry me back to bed. My brave, sweet, loving mother. I felt my heart break for her in empathy… and I knew. I knew that she had felt what I had felt, and she had hurt how I was hurting, and I had never been more connected to her in my entire life. I remembered the Christmas that dad wasn't home, and mom had told us that he was working. I remembered and knew that it was true. It was all true. All of the things she told me were real.

She went on to tell me that Dad had promised it would never happen again, and that he would be the perfect husband. That he'd realized what he'd done, that he couldn't lose his family, and that he would never, ever take us for granted again. Not ever.

"I let him come home, Mand. But it took me five years to trust him again. And ten years to love him. I won't tell you that it was easy. It was so, so hard."

I listened and absorbed and integrated what was an entirely new reality to me.

"But," she said, "I just want you to know, he wasn't lying. He never did it again. And he did become a wonderful husband and father. He still is. I'll always be sad that he cheated on me, Mandy… but I think he needed to. I think he had to cheat to know what matters. Maybe Brock could be that way too."

It was then that I realized — I didn't know my parents when they were new. I only knew the older, more mature parents that had already been through the gauntlet of youth and stupidity. My image of them was not a sham, just an incomplete picture; a fragment of the entirety of their big, brilliant, beautiful, painful reality. I had somehow convinced myself that marriage, despite my relationship with Jonas, was only the good stuff. That, if there was true love, there would be no hard times. Love meant there could be no struggle nor turmoil nor pain.

My mother's story, the pain and the betrayal and the growth and the forgiveness, opened up for me a whole new possibility—that people who truly loved each other could also truly struggle. I was surprised to learn that there might be something there underneath all of the kindness and sweetness and joy—that maybe the seed of true partnership was buried in the soil of strife. Perhaps the bloom of compassion grew out of shared pain. That maybe, just maybe, in order to flourish together, we first had to fail together.

I thanked my mother whole-heartedly, and told her that I loved her deeply, and then hung up the phone. I sat in silence in my car for a while. Mom hadn't told me what to do, but she had told me some deep, hard truth, and I suddenly knew with crystal clarity what I was going to choose. I turned on the car, and I drove home. I hadn't made it past that gas station. I walked through the front door and into Brock's surprised arms. We held each other tightly as we both cried and kissed and gently murmured promises to figure it out, to get through it together, to make it right. I knew we had something worth saving, and I was willing to put in the work, as long as he was too.

chapter 5

When Brock, several months later, proposed marriage, I was immediately irritated. I had already been married once, and that didn't work. I wasn't planning to ever get married again, and I had told Brock that several times. Marriage was a sham. We didn't have to do anything formal. We could just keep hanging out together as long as it made both of us happy. I still wanted children. Some part of me still wanted that perfection I had always dreamed of. But I was also worried that Brock was just managing his inclination only for so long as losing me was a risk, and that he would go right back to pornography as soon as I was securely his.

I said no.

No, thank you.

I did, however, still want to have babies. Babies without marriage…what would be the big deal? Raising kids was going to be easy, and fun. We didn't have to do that stupid, expensive wedding thing in order to have children. So, even though I said no to Brock's marriage proposal, I began telling him as often as I possibly could that I wanted to get pregnant. I wanted a baby. I couldn't wait to start. He would laugh at me, and kiss me, and tell me he wanted to be married first. It was a standoff.

Brock really believed in marriage. He really *wanted* to be married. And he didn't want to have kids outside of marriage. So he kept asking. And asking. And asking. It wasn't a proposal each time—he never got down on one knee. He just sprinkled little probing offers throughout our days. 'Hey, we need a new mattress. I have enough money for a new bed, or for an engagement ring. Which one should I get?' 'Hey, I was going to swing by the jewelry store tonight and buy a ring for you. Sound good?' 'Do you want to pick out engagement rings with me tonight? I'm ready to propose if you are ready to let me.' He really wanted to get married, and he really wanted to marry *me*. I thought he was crazy.

One afternoon, after we had been happily cohabitating for just over a year, and after something like eight or nine declined marriage requests, we went to spend the day at Brock's parents' house. Judy and Tim lived in a big, golden, gorgeous home on Lake Norman, and I loved being there. They had built it themselves, and Brock grew up there, on the water, overlooking the lake. As much as I missed my family, living so far away from home, hanging out with Brock's parents felt like a close second.

We pulled into the driveway as the sun was shining through the trees, and the wind was fluttering the leaves. I was so grateful to be there, and looking forward to a beautiful day on the water. We unloaded the car, and Brock walked up to the front door just as his mother Judy stepped out to greet us. Judy hugged Brock, and then pushed him in the house, and closed the door behind him. She stepped in front of the door and turned towards me. She had a plan.

Still diminutive, but with a massive personality, Judy turned her crystal-blue eyes on me, and reminiscent of our original unexpected wedding conversation, Judy bluntly stated, "Brock really wants to marry you."

I thought I could no longer be surprised by Judy, but my eyes jumped wide open.

"I... I know he does,' I stuttered. I felt like I needed to defend myself. 'I just... I don't really want to do that again." My shoulders slumped in shame. I looked everywhere but directly at her. I had failed at being married. I didn't need to fail again. I didn't think my self-esteem could handle it.

She stepped into my line of sight, and grabbed my hand to hold me in place. "Mandy," she began gently, "*Brock* wants to get married. He believes in marriage. I know that your first marriage didn't work out, but you can't punish Brock for that. He's an old fashioned guy… he won't do it any other way." She paused and looked at me with an intensity that froze me. "If you aren't going to marry him, you have to let him go."

The finality of her words resounded throughout my whole being. I hadn't thought of it that way before, and suddenly I began looking at things differently. There had been no more issues with porn, or any other girls, or jealousy, or even video games. I really was punishing Brock for the mistakes Jonas had made, and that wasn't fair. Over the next few days and weeks, I started to allow myself to think about getting married, and what that could look like.

The next time Brock asked me to marry him, officially, and with a ring, I said yes.

In July the following year, Brock and I were married in a beautiful chapel at the corner of Williamson and Brawley School Road. We drove away from our ceremony in my little blue Mini Cooper, and headed to our reception. It was a perfect, bright, sun-shiny day. The reception was to take place at Brock's parents house, and Judy and Tim lovingly welcomed me into the fold. We had invited all of our closest friends, and a few beloved co-workers, but it was a tiny affair. My family drove all the way down from Canada, and we were surrounded by so much love. Our wedding photos show us happily smiling and dancing on the boardwalk, joyful at the beginning of our new life together.

What the pictures don't show, however, is that I was already, unexpectedly, seven weeks pregnant.

Two weeks before our wedding day I was late for my period. I was stressed out, and feeling yucky, and completely anxious about the wedding we had been planning that was just fourteen days away. I had a to-do list a mile long, and I couldn't imagine doing any of it. I was sick. I was exhausted. I was just not okay.

In a moment of wild inspiration, I wondered if I should take a pregnancy test. I knew it was highly unlikely that I would be pregnant... I had *just* stopped taking my birth control in preparation for being married, and it was going to take a long time for all of those hormones to clear out of my system. I'd been working ultrasound for a while, and I knew the rates of infertility. I knew how hard women had to try to get pregnant.

Brock was at work, and I was alone. I didn't really want to test without him, but I also couldn't shake the thought once it came to me. There was absolutely no way I was going to be able to wait five more hours and have him stop and get a test on the way home. My to-do list completely forgotten, I got in my car and drove to the nearest drug store. I stood in front of the pregnancy test section, unsure what to look for or which test to buy. I had never done it before. *Do I get a digital one? Holy crap, these are expensive. Do the ones that cost more do a better job??* I was completely out of my depth, and didn't want to waste a ton of money on what was probably a long shot. I wasn't going to get pregnant. I was barren. I knew it. I had worried about it my whole life.

With a flush of irritation, I reached out and grabbed the cheapest, no-name brand two-pack of pregnancy tests on the shelf, and hurried up to the checkout counter. I briefly toyed with the idea of peeing on the stick right there in the drugstore bathroom, but decided that I wanted to be in the safety of my own home before I peed on anything.

I raced back home with a full bladder, and stalked straight into the bathroom. I didn't even bother to read the directions—I figured it was pretty simple... hold the absorbent side underneath your bottom, and then pee on it.

I peed on it.

Then I put it down, and walked away. I wasn't really ready to know what it said. On the one hand, it was possible that it was going to say that I was pregnant, and I wouldn't believe it, because holy cow I'd wanted to be pregnant forever, and that would be incredible and-but-also it would totally ruin my wedding, and somehow we had gotten pregnant out of wedlock, and what the heck was I doing??

On the other hand, it would probably be negative, and that would be hard. It would be really hard to get my hopes up, and wonder and worry and wish and then find out that I was not pregnant. I braced myself for a big fat no.

I walked into the kitchen and set a timer on the microwave for five minutes. I wasn't going to walk back into the bathroom until the timer was beeping. I took a deep breath, and stilled my body, and tried to focus on being calm, relaxed, peaceful... I looked up at the timer that said 4:46, said "Fuck it," and ran back into the bathroom and picked up the test.

It was positive.

Positive. It was positive. Completely impossible. *How is this possible?!* It couldn't be correct, and my brain refused to accept the two little lines in front of me, so I pulled out the second test. I didn't know I was going to need the second test, and yet here it was. But my bladder was empty, and I was in shock.

I stormed back out into the kitchen and filled a glass of water. I gulped it out of shaking hands, and looked back at the clock on the microwave. The timer was still running down and said 3:32. It had been less than two minutes. There was no way I was going to be able to go pee again. I paced back and forth from one side of my kitchen to the other, willing the water to hit my bladder as soon as possible. Patience has never, not ever, been a single one of my strong suits, and before the original timer even started beeping, I hurried back into the toilet and decided to just try to *squeeze some out.*

I really didn't know how much pee it took to run a pregnancy test, but apparently a dribble was plenty, because this time, I pulled up the stick and looked at it immediately, and it had already started turning positive.

Holy fucking shit, I am pregnant.

I suddenly realized that the emotion that I was feeling wasn't fear or consternation, nor was it excitement or joy.

It was *relief.*

All of the years spent worrying and wishing and dreaming about being a mother had always stayed overwritten by the fear of never being able to conceive, and here I was, albeit a little on the early side, pregnant with my first child. I was going to have a baby!

I was immediately so excited, and ready to bask in the joy and ecstasy of creating new life. Pregnancy was going to be dreamy. I just knew it.

Only, it was NOT dreamy.

There was no part of it that was dreamy. Dreamy couldn't be farther from the way I would describe the experience.

It was awful.

Within days, I hated being pregnant so badly. The changes in my body were almost immediate. Morning sickness was a joke—I was sick all day long. I could no longer eat the food that I wanted without feeling completely nauseated. I thought I would have some time, but I wasn't even two months pregnant and already I couldn't stand the feeling of pressure on my abdomen. I was uncomfortably crampy, and sure that it couldn't possibly be normal. Everything felt *moist.* It was so gross. I was miserable all of the time. There I was, smack dab in the middle of exactly what I had always dreamed of, and instead of elated, I was disgusted. Anxious. Irritated. Disappointed.

In addition to my unexpectedly awful experience of actually being pregnant, Brock was not as elated to be becoming a father as I thought he should be. He had wanted to wait for a few years before having children. He wanted to get to spend time together as a couple before we added children to the equation.

One evening, we were laying on the couch talking about our day, and I changed the subject without much notice. "What do you think is going to be the greatest part of being a dad?" Brock shook his head gently in confusion, and answered abruptly, "I don't know." He sounded tight and snappy, and immediately something clenched in my stomach. He was supposed to be excited. We were having a child. I couldn't understand why he felt irritated, or what I had done wrong. "Don't you want to have a baby, Brock? Aren't you excited?" I could feel myself getting upset—hormones prob-ably—but also, I just didn't want anything to be wrong. I wanted him to want this baby, too.

He paused a moment, and then leaned over towards me and put his hands on my cheek. "Of course I want this baby, Mandy. And I'm trying to figure out how to be excited." His eyes got a far off look. "You have to understand, babe… my whole childhood, all anyone ever told me was how having a kid would ruin my life." My eyes widened with surprise. He was right, I knew he was. That's what everyone says—don't have kids too early, it will ruin your life. He looked me in the eyes and his were sparkling with humor, "You'll have to give me some time. It is kind of hard to switch from *this will ruin your life* to *this is the best thing ever.*"

And so, several months later, finally married and essentially ready, our first child was born as most American babies are: in a hospital under the care of an Obstetrician-Gynecologist. For all intents and purposes, it was a perfect birth; a scheduled induction at 39 weeks so the baby wouldn't get too big, pitocin to make sure contractions were nice and strong, epidural to keep me comfortable. From the time we walked into the hospital, until the doctor told me it was time to push, a scant six hours had passed. It wasn't what I had expected—truly, I thought I would labor for hours, maybe days—but I found myself surprised and a little bit swept away by the suddenness of the announcement—*It's time to push already??*

I was coached through pushing, and apparently did a good job, as I watched in the birth mirror that I had requested and saw the head of my son be born out of my body (I did not feel anything). Then I burst IMMEDIATELY into tears of joy as he rotated in the birth canal, and I caught a glimpse of his beautiful face. Another push, and he was born, and I loved him so much. Already, I loved him so much. Immediately. This part was exactly what I had dreamed it would be. Brilliance. A boy. My son. Our Ronan.

Having a baby was the biggest bait-and-switch I could possibly have imagined. In my mind, for my entire life, being a new mother was peace and sunshine and rainbows and laughter and joy… not screaming, and frustration and terror and tears. (Most of them mine). Don't get me wrong, I loved Ronan with my whole entire heart and thought he was each and every little bit of worldly magic rolled up into one tiny perfect human. But it was hard. I think no one had ever taken the time to tell me how absolutely fucking terrifying it is to mother a newborn baby. Maybe they did, and I just didn't listen. Anyways, the dreamy haze of my beautiful new boy wore off pretty quickly in the fog of sore nipples and blown-out diapers and absolutely. Zero. Sleep.

It was harder than I thought it could be, and harder than I wanted to be, and I was angry about it. I was also sad, lonely, and frustrated. I didn't have any friends that had had children yet, and I had no idea how to go about finding some. My mom didn't come to help. Judy wasn't particularly maternal, and didn't seem willing to help. Brock was willing to help with anything he could, and mostly I just didn't even know what I needed.

The first months of Ronan's life were marked with a darkness, a haze that I had not expected. I found myself mired in a postpartum depression that I did not recognize at that time. And as much as Brock loved his sweet baby boy, he wasn't the most immediate nor natural of fathers. It came pretty easily to him to let me do most of the chores, and most of the night time parenting, most of the feeding, most of the cooking… well, really, most of everything. He loved us, and cared about us, and was generally just sweet and wonderful. But even though the weight of motherhood was crushing me, taking some of that burden on as his own never seemed to occur to him. He was well-rested and well-fed and spry while I was fading away into a shadow of the woman I had just barely known before becoming a mom.

There were so many wonderful firsts that I wasn't patient enough to wait for. When would he first smile? When would he roll over? When will he get his first tooth? When will he walk, talk, run? I was so impatient for all of the milestones, that I hardly enjoyed a minute of what we had. I wasn't really present for any of it—I was constantly rushing from one thing to the next, barely holding still, and also beating myself up constantly for not loving every second.

I would also like to add that quite literally every single thing I said I would never do before I became a parent (and was therefore a *perfect parent*) we ended up doing in spades. Crappy plastic toys, TV as a babysitter, tantrums in public, bed-sharing... all of it. Child-free me owed every single parent on the face of the planet an apology for being such a stuck-up bitch. That big ol' helping of humble pie sure went down rough.

My memories of Ronan's first year consisted of the hours of the day that were spent simply meeting the immediate physical needs of my child, and not much else. Not even meeting my own needs. I was so out of my depth. I felt lost. Like I was looking up at the surface and unsure how to get there. When I look back at pictures of baby Ronan, I see smiles and beauty and joy, but they are also marked with a sadness, and I still feel a heavy guilt that it wasn't all love and light. It was hard, and sometimes I hated it.

Despite the darkness and struggle, my days as an unhappy mother turned into weeks, which turned into months and we managed to keep going. Without fully understanding how, Brock and Ronan and I muscled through that first year. It took a full year, but eventually, I started to hit my stride as a mother, and adjusted to the loss of my identity as a person, the loss of my *self*, and started to accept that that was my life, and I could do it. I was *mom*.

And, of course, as one does when one is as-yet still immature and completely un-self-aware, I eventually decided that having another baby was the next right thing. You know, despite my first experience being pregnant and slogging through the newborn stage, and still being alone and lonely within the walls of my home. Definitely, absolutely, without a doubt, one more baby would fix it.

chapter 6

My cycle came back when Ronan was about 9 months old, and while Brock and I hadn't explicitly discussed trying for another baby, we were also not exactly careful when it came to contraception either. We had always discussed that we wanted our kids to be about 2 years apart (three children total), and so it seemed like a good time for me to stop reminding Brock to 'be careful'.

I still wasn't fully convinced that, despite my prior fertility, I would get pregnant immediately—and yet I did. One morning in early February, about the time that I was expecting my next period to start, I had an inkling and took a pregnancy test. It was a fast positive. I had to go to work that evening, and was riding high on the thrill of the future, and another baby, and getting a second try at this 'perfect life' dream I'd been holding on to.

Since having Ronan, I had gotten a job working as an emergency room Ultrasound Tech—weekend overnights at a nearby hospital, and was there by myself from 11pm until 7am. I arrived at work glowing, and floated through the halls. It was too early, of course, to tell anyone so I walked around with my bright little secret squirreled away under my heart. *Another baby!*

It was around midnight when I first felt a small gush of blood. I knew, almost immediately, what it meant. My heart sank. The pregnancy was over—short and bittersweet, wanted and anticipated but unable to stay. I sat in the bathroom of the Ultrasound department under the glaring fluorescent lights and miscarried into the toilet and cried into my hands. Having no other choice, I got up and went back to work.

No one knew, not even Brock, and it was so wildly alone and lonely.

Since I had been pregnant for just a moment, and hardly long enough to tell, I wasn't completely destroyed by the loss. I could have been. That fear that I had carried through my childhood, it was still there simmering under the surface. I didn't want to let it be real, and I didn't want to look at it. *Lots of women have miscarriages*, I told myself. *They can be totally normal.* Instead of spiraling down into heartbreak, I chalked my loss up to my hormones being off, and not leaving enough time for my cycle to re-establish. I didn't let myself go too deep, too dark. I told Brock the following morning that I had had a miscarriage, and he was so lovely and comforting. He instinctively seemed to understand how hard it was to feel even that tiny-and-yet-so-huge loss. We agreed to try again in earnest the next month.

True to form, in March, I peed on a stick at the appropriate time, and celebrated the euphoria of yet another positive test. I laughed at myself and all of the years I had wasted worrying and worrying about not being able to get pregnant—fertility was not one of the things my husband and I were destined to struggle with. Even better, this baby seemed bound to stay!

I made it past the 6th week of pregnancy with no bleeding. I stopped holding my breath every single time I sat down to pee, and was still pregnant through the 7th and 8th weeks of gestation. My symptoms had been growing steadily stronger and stronger, and eventually I was nauseated most of the day, with achy boobs and powerful food aversions. I was comforted by the symptoms that had so irritated me in my first pregnancy—they meant that I was still pregnant.

As I neared the 9th week of pregnancy, I woke up early one morning and felt wonderful.

Wonderful.

I gasped and immediately my lower belly clenched in fear.

Wonderful, not nauseated. Wonderful, not tender. Wonderful, not exhausted.

Fuck.

I laid in bed for a while and attempted to summon the morning sickness. There was a possibility that I just wasn't paying enough attention, and everything was fine. Feeling wonderful didn't have to mean anything. I tried not to let myself worry, and hoped that my symptoms would jump me with a vengeance as soon as I got my day started. I rolled out of bed… and felt fine. I went through the motions of our mom-and-toddler morning routine, made breakfast for the two of us… and felt fine. I got myself dressed, pulled my shirt down over my head… and I felt fine. I decided that I needed to get out of the house and out of my head. I called a friend and asked her if she wanted to meet at the mall to chat and let the kids play. I did not tell her that I was pregnant, nor that I was worried.

I packed Ronan and the diaper bag into the car and drove around the corner to the local mall. I parked, and gripped my hands tightly on the wheel, and took a deep breath. I tried to clear my mind of the worry, and just be present, in the moment, with myself and my son. There was no reason, yet, why we couldn't enjoy our day. I firmed my resolve, got out of the car and walked around to Ronan's car seat. I unbuckled him and grunted as I worked to lift him out of his place. As I strained my muscles, I felt a gush, and I knew right then that life was gone. I gently cried out, "Oh," and tears filled my eyes as I apologized to Ronan and buckled him back into his seat, and then went home to lose another baby.

The miscarriage was much worse this time. Much more blood, and infinitely more pain. I called my OB/GYN office and asked the nurse what I should do. She told me that it was safe to stay home as long as I was managing my pain, and the bleeding wasn't too severe, but that I could always go in to the ER.

I'd been working in the ER for the last several months, and because of that, I decided that I would not go in. I knew there was nothing they could do for me. As an ultrasound tech, I had always felt so powerless during miscarriages. Not that I didn't want to try to help, to ease the pain or the suffering, but there was really nothing I could do. It hadn't taken me terribly long as an ultrasound tech to get jaded enough to wish that people wouldn't come in for early pregnancy loss. I even went so far as to think, when scanning a threatened miscarriage, "Why are you here? There is nothing we can do for you."

I had those thoughts right up until the day I had my second miscarriage. It wasn't just the bleeding or the pain that mattered. Those weren't the only parts of a miscarriage that counted or deserved to be recognized. They definitely weren't the only reasons a person might consider going into the hospital. I had never considered before that there was also the heart, and the soul, and the emotion; the heartache and the fear; the wondering and the worrying. *Is this normal? Am I okay? I don't want to do this alone.*

Sitting at home, losing my baby and wrapped up in more than just bleeding and pain was the loneliest feeling that I had yet experienced. Brock was there with me, but he didn't get it. He couldn't. It wasn't his job to carry a baby. It was mine. And I was failing. Again.

I wasn't just sad this time. I was disappointed, ashamed, and afraid. Disappointed to be losing another baby that we so desperately wanted, ashamed that my body didn't seem to be able to carry another pregnancy, and afraid that I would never have another child.

From that moment forward, I never, ever wondered again why a woman might show up at the emergency room, sad and scared and worried that she might be losing her baby.

After my second miscarriage, Brock and I decided to stop trying to get pregnant for a while. It didn't make sense for us to keep going through loss when it appeared that my body wasn't capable of supporting new life. I wasn't sure my mental health would be able to support me much longer either. I had already been depressed and lonely, and after two back-to-back miscarriages, I sunk so deeply into the most intense darkness, I completely lost touch with the light. I stopped reaching out to friends. I didn't do anything for fun. I went through the motions, meeting Ronan's needs and just barely taking care of myself.

Wake, live, sleep. Day after day.

Brock held me and supported me and tried to assist in any way that he could, coming home early and missing work to care for Ronan, to care for me, but I was unreachable. I was grieving my lost babies, and the big, beautiful family I had hoped for. I was longing for all of the joy I had imagined that I would feel within the life I had been dreaming of but did not have. I was mourning my childhood dream of marriage and children and perfection. Miscarriages were my first real, true, deep experience with grief. While I had lost grandparents, and I was sad that they had died, I didn't have that experience of visceral loss. Of being bereft. Of the magnitude of the "you are gone from me," feeling. My grandparents were supposed to die. They were old, and that was how life worked. I was not supposed to lose my babies.

After weeks of feeling miserable and low, and actually quite ill, it finally occurred to me to take another pregnancy test. Maybe I was sick and sad and low for a reason? I peed on another stick and stared as it turned immediately positive.

I was not trying to be pregnant. We were not trying to get pregnant. I didn't want to get my hopes up or be hopeful or even wishful at all. I wasn't elated. I wasn't relieved.

I was terrified.

This cannot be happening.

I would not let myself get connected to the baby. I was so hesitant to love or even long for that little spirit, and I didn't tell anyone, not even Brock. For days and days, all I did was wait for the worst. Every time I went to pee, I prepared to see blood. I started dreading going to the bathroom. Every time I picked up anything even remotely heavy, I braced to feel a gush. Every morning that I woke up, I readied myself to say goodbye. It was so, so exhausting to be so constantly waiting to grieve again.

But days just kept passing, and against the odds, I was still pregnant. Weeks passed. Then months. Every morning I woke up feeling miserable was another day I was surprisingly 'with child'. By the time I made it to my fourth month and had still not started bleeding, I finally told Brock I was pregnant, and we began to hope that maybe this baby would stay, together.

As I began to believe that the baby would stay, another strange thing happened, something I had never expected: I found myself looking entirely differently at the symptoms of pregnancy. I was completely changed. I had loathed being pregnant with Ronan, had hated the experience so much that all of the symptoms had frustrated and irritated and enraged me. But, much like sunshine after a cold night can melt the frost, the fact that I was not losing this babe shone like a bright, warm ray. Cramps and aches? Still pregnant! Exhausted and moody? That means I'm pregnant! Moist and uncomfortable? Hey, guess who's PREGNANT??

Because of my miscarriages, because I had lost so much, I was finally, finally able to enjoy the signs, symptoms and realities of pregnancy that I had hated so much the first time around. They weren't different or better in any way at all. I was *just so fucking thankful* that the baby had decided to stay, and I was willing to put up with and live through absolutely anything to get to keep one.

As my belly grew, so did my discomfort, and yet I stayed so unbelievably thankful to get to continue carrying my sweet babe. Every ache and pain was just as beautiful to me as every kick and tumble. Gratitude took what I had hated before, and turned it into enough. Into more than enough. Into the biggest blessing I could imagine.

I drank deeply of that gratitude and was truly glowing as I approached the 39th week of pregnancy. This time around, I was determined not to rush. Unlike with Ronan, I didn't want to be induced, and I was willing to stay pregnant until I went into labor on my own. I wanted to revel in every last moment, and steep in the beauty of holding my baby safe within my womb.

I woke up on the morning of February 9th, just a few days shy of my Valentine's due date, feeling uncomfortable, and large, and unbeautifully ungainly. I truly believe that pregnancy has to get uncomfortable at the end so that one is willing to face the crucible of birth because there is NO WAY anyone would be willing to stay pregnant and miserable forever. At some critical point, childbirth begins to feel like the better option.

I rolled out of bed when I could hear Ronan nattering to himself on the baby monitor, and smiled at his adorable toddler sounds as I slowly waddled up the stairs to get him. I braced my big belly as I strained to pull him out of his crib, hugged him into me, and then immediately set him on the floor. He was solidly twenty-five pounds, and also deep enough into toddlerhood that he wanted to do EVERYTHING himself, such that carrying him down the stairs just wasn't an option for either of us.

We paused at the top of the stairs, and I set one foot down onto the first tread. I turned back to hold Ronan's hand and guide him down; the stairs were steep, and carpeted, and felt treacherous. He pulled away from me, as he wanted to do it alone, but I insisted he hold my hand. Only, as I leaned farther to reach for him again, my weight shifted too far back in my body, and my foot (that was placed too close to the end of the step) slipped out from underneath me. It was so fast, and so unexpected. My heel just glanced off the end of the stair. And even though it was so fast, in my head it happened in slow motion, all of my thoughts crystal clear, and discreet, and visceral.

Oh shit. I'm falling.

I let out a loud wail of fear, and felt as gravity worked on my bulk, and my giant pregnant ass hurtled down towards the step I had just left.

This is really going to hurt.

My tailbone slammed into the carpet covered board and I felt a snap, an instant of sharp, searing pain. That could have been it, and it would have been enough, but gravity didn't ease up, and momentum had its hold on me. There was nothing for my flailing hands to grab on to. In a rush, a tumble, I slid down the length of the entire stairway and landed in a crumpled heap at the bottom.

The baby. Oh god, the baby.

I felt pain and fear everywhere. I could hear Ronan crying out desperately from the top of the stairs. I don't know if it was watching me fall that was terrifying, or hearing the sounds that I had made, but he was hysterical.

Brock heard my yell along with a grand series of thuds, and came rushing out from the bathroom where he was getting ready for work. He tried to pull on me—desperate to help me up and make sure I was okay.

"Go get Ronan first—I'm okay. Go get Ronan."

I took a few breaths as my tears slowed down to calm myself, and check in. Was I okay? Did I break anything??

Is the baby okay?

I leveraged myself into a sitting position as Brock came back down with Ronan, and felt a stabbing pain like hot coals in my tailbone. I cried out again, and was immediately sure that I had broken something. But I really, really wasn't concerned about myself, or my tailbone, or the pain. I was just so worried about the baby.

I leaned forward, and held completely still, hands on my belly, wishing, waiting, willing to feel my baby move so that I would know that everyone was okay. I tried to tune out Brock, who was crooning to Ronan and holding him close to me so I could reassure him. But I couldn't. I wiped the tears off of my cheeks, then pressed both hands firmly into my swollen abdomen, and focused deeply, deeply into myself.

Please let me know you are okay, baby. Please.

I waited for what felt like an eternity, and then looked up at Brock in horror.

"The baby's not moving. I can't feel the baby move. Brock, I don't know what to do. What do we do? Should we go to the hospital??"

I started to feel frantic. My chest tightened, and my throat constricted, and the tears jumped into my eyes unbidden. I could not lose this baby too. I couldn't. I wouldn't survive it.

Brock called our friend Laura on my phone and asked if we could drop Ronan off for a few hours. We immediately loaded into the car, left Ronan at Laura's house, and then headed to the emergency room.

I couldn't take a full breath. Everything was wrong. I couldn't get out of my head.

Please be okay. Please be okay. Oh sweet baby, please stay.

When we walked up to the desk, I broke out in sobs as I explained that I was 39 weeks pregnant, I had fallen down the stairs, and I hadn't felt the baby move since.

They brought me back into triage right away, and put me on a stretcher to try to find a heartbeat. The nurses hands were shaking a little as she applied the jelly and then the little heart-rate disk. She tried on the left side of my belly, and murmured little reassuring nothings as she tried to find the sound. My eyes were tightly closed—I couldn't look. I couldn't look at Brock, and I definitely could not look at the nurse. I had my eyes clenched shut, and felt the entirety of the weight of the terror in my chest as I waited to hear whether or not my baby was still alive.

Please. Please. Please.

The nurse pulled the monitor away from my belly with a loud squeal, and squirted some more jelly, then tried the other side, the right side. My muscles tensed tighter and tighter as I braced myself to hear the news I was sure she was about to give me.

Slide up, push, slide down, push, angle, angle… *whump whump whump whump.*

There! It was there, the heartbeat was there.

I collapsed, my entire body unclenched into tears of relief, and Brock held me as we cried out our gratitude.

The baby stayed.
The baby stayed.
The baby stayed.

The baby was born the following morning, after the tumble down the stairs led to labor. The baby was a daughter! The entire world stopped for an instant when she was born, roared out in a birthing center after 6 hours of labor and one powerful push. Everything paused for just a moment as she slowly blinked her beautiful eyes, and let out her answering cry—"I'm here," her sweet wail said, and she was. All of creation seemed to freeze for one fraction of a second as the universe welcomed our gorgeous, tender, tiny, precious girl. In a flash, she was born, and life before her ceased to have any meaning at all. It was as though everything alive and good and beautiful in the world knew that it had all been changed for the better. And it was. Because Ruby Kate was born.

chapter 7

Ruby was a colicky baby, and we struggled to breastfeed. Despite my triumphant birth and joy that she had stayed, her piercing screams and trouble nursing played havoc on my tenuous mental health. Ronan was just newly two when started seeing signs of speech and sensory delays, and Ruby just cried and cried. I had never been a stellar house-keeper; I struggled with basic maintenance, and keeping the house clean with a toddler and a newborn was an absolute nightmare. Our home was usually barely a step or two above biohazard, and on every single level of my life—mothering, wife-ing, keeping house—I was failing disastrously and ravaging myself because of it.

Beyond that, for the weeks leading up to Ruby's birth, Brock was struggling at work. There were some employees at his office that were acting unprofessionally towards the women he worked with, and when he brought it up to the management, they dismissed his concerns. All of his pent up anger and irritation and frustration came home with him every single day. It was bleeding over into our family life and we were all miserable about it. We agreed that the best course of action was for him to find a new job, but that the quickest way for him to exit the damaging situation was for him to just quit. I was hoping that that meant he would be more helpful with Ronan as I was trying to deal with colicky, not-breastfeeding Ruby. I fully expected him to take a week or two of decompressing and lounging before he buckled down into finding new work. When those weeks turned into months, things started crumbling even more quickly than before. Not just our living situation, but also our financial situation, and ultimately, our marriage.

We ended up having to move in with Brock's parents. Their beautiful house on the lake—it wasn't immediately a hardship. I felt lucky to have that option open to us. I figured I would have some help with the kids, and all of the housework and cooking and parenting wouldn't rest solely on me. We rented out our sweet little townhome so we wouldn't have to sell it, and I kept working my weekend ultrasound job to keep health insurance and fund our expenses while Brock looked for work.

Or rather, did not look.

I may not ever fully know what went on within Brock's mind and soul during that time, but he ceased functioning as a human being. He fell deeply into video games and social media and television. He didn't participate in parenting, nor house-keeping, nor family activities. He loved his kids, and he loved me, but he really wasn't *doing* anything. Even a person such as myself, deeply loving and empathetic and helpful, can tolerate that behavior for a little while, but not forever.

I felt myself going absolutely insane. Still thoroughly struggling with the darkness in my mind and my heart, and living in the basement of Brock's somewhat-judgy and type-A parents, I was never doing enough. The house was never *clean* enough, my kids were never *quiet* enough, the food I cooked was never nutritious enough. And in the very same moment, in many ways I was too much; the things that mattered to me were obnoxious, and my rules against and treats for my kids were ridiculous, and my choice to cosleep was abhorrent. The help I had imagined never materialized, and my mother-in-law even canceled her weekly housekeeper, leaving *more* of the burden on my shoulders. My mental health was already in a tenuous place when we moved in, and I was slowly ground down beneath the heel of unsupportive, un-caring, un-empathetic in-laws. It was me against everyone else, and I was losing.

I became short and waspish, cold and unwelcoming. I started pulling away from everyone, and kept to myself. I stopped trying to help out or visit with or communicate to anyone in the household. I found myself unable to care at all about what my husband was going through or what my in-laws thought. I lost touch with any compassion and all empathy for myself, my husband, and even my kids. As my mood got darker and darker, and my thoughts blacker and meaner, I eventually started looking for the escape hatch. In my free time, I started looking for affordable apartments—if I was doing everything on my own, I might as well actually be *on my own*.

The last and final straw came one evening in September when Ruby was seven months old. I sat down at the computer to write an entry in my blog, and for some strange reason, I felt undeniably compelled to hit Ctrl-Z. If you are not familiar with common PC usage, Ctrl-Z is the 'undo' function, which will immediately reverse whatever was the last action done on the computer. To be honest, I had not thought of nor worried about pornography since before our wedding. I believed that Brock and I had that beast thoroughly beaten, and it was not a constant worry for me. I hadn't even really taken it seriously as I hit the buttons. It took my brain a second to catch up to the reality that a pornographic video file was un-deleted and replaced itself on the desktop.

ARE YOU FUCKING KIDDING ME?

My entire body flushed with heat and hatred. Here, this man was not helping. Not cooking. Not cleaning. Not parenting. Not doing anything at all to help or be a part of our lives, and yet still expecting me to have sex with him regularly. No job. No grocery shopping. No washing the cars or reading to the kids. He couldn't do any of that, but he somehow had found time for PORN again??

I was absolutely fucking devastated, and yet I couldn't access any of my emotions. I couldn't cry. I couldn't yell. I couldn't even find my way to the anger that was burning like fire inside of me. Somewhere, over the last several months, I had become so disconnected from my body that I was completely numb.

All I knew was that I wanted out.

Out of that toxic fucking household, out from under my over-sexed and under-matured husband, out of the whole fucking marriage and reality and life.

That night, I sat next to Brock on the couch and told him, deadpan and emotionless, that I was leaving. I told him without even a hint of affect that I didn't love him any more, and what was worse than that, I didn't even like him anymore. I told him that I had found the porn, and that I was disgusted and disappointed in him as a person, and I was absolutely fucking miserable living in his parents house. I told him it was all his fault.

Without stuttering or hesitating, I informed him that I was going to file for divorce, and I was taking our children and moving back to Canada to live with my parents. *At least there*, I thought, *I will be loved and supported and cared for, and not entirely alone.*

Brock's reaction was predictable and true-to-form. He immediately cried and begged and apologized. He said lots of sweet sounding bullshit about how he'd lost himself, and was just so broken, and how he wanted to get better. He wanted to fix things. He'd see a therapist with me, a marriage counselor.

"I can get better, Mandy. I can be better. Please don't leave me."

My mind flashed back to what my mother had said about some guys needing to do the wrong things, but my heart was cold and closed, and I declined; I informed him that that ship had sailed long ago. I did not comfort him, nor soften my resolve. I was not the cause of his pain, I realized. I was just no longer allowing him to hurt me instead. I had my vows.

When he finally grasped that I was serious, that I was not going to bend, that this was the only path forward that I was willing to take, he very pitifully asked if he could make love to me just one last time. Our sexual chemistry and connection in the bedroom had never been an issue, and I did have a smidgeon of pity for him, so I said sure.

Why not? I'll engage in a final pity fuck. What is the worst that could happen?

Unsurprisingly, the worst that could happen happened when I turned up pregnant two weeks later. I was not happy to be pregnant. I was devastated. I DID NOT want to remain married to that useless man just because I was pregnant with another one of his children. I DID NOT want to be a single mother to three kids, nor go through pregnancy and childbirth by myself. *Holy fucking shit*, I realized, *I have no good options.*

In a rush of mad desperation, and only four weeks pregnant, I scheduled an abortion. I didn't even want Brock to know about the baby, because I wasn't keeping it. I put the date on the calendar, and refused to know or connect to the life within me in any meaningful way. It was not going to be the reason I relented and stayed.

The day before the scheduled procedure, I was called with a pre-op questionnaire and instructions, which included the requirement that I had to have someone with me to drop me off and pick me up. I froze, stuttering as my mind raced to think of someone that I could ask to be that person for me, and it was blank. There was no one. Brock was my only person. I didn't have a single friend or acquaintance that I could ask to be the one to drive me home from something so hard. Through tears of frustration, I told the lady on the phone to cancel the procedure. I wasn't going to go through with it.

Just because I didn't have a fucking ride.

I had not thought it was possible for me to sink lower into depression and desolation, but I felt sure that I was finally at rock-bottom. I was alone, and lonely, and completely cut off from any loving or caring connection, any tethering to life. I put the phone down and dejectedly walked into the bathroom to inform Brock that I was pregnant with his child, and collapsed in tears on the floor.

I heard a gasp, and when I looked up at his face, Brock's eyes were filled with tears and bright with joy at the news. I paused, snuffled and caught my breath. "You're happy? You're happy that I'm pregnant?"

Brock pulled me up off the floor and scooped me up into a tight hug that I held myself rigid against.

"Of course I'm happy! Mandy, please… give me a chance. This is a sign. Let me prove it to you that I can be worthy of you, and our family, and this baby. This gift." He squeezed me tightly and spoke into the top of my head. "Oh Mandy. Please."

I pushed myself out of his arms and turned away. I hadn't experienced a smidge of softening. I was angry. Enraged that I was pregnant, and indignant that he thought this was a blessing, "his chance." I was absolutely incensed that I even had to deal with any of this bullshit. I was leaving. I already had plane tickets for myself and the kids. Passports were ready. In two weeks, we were flying to Canada, where I was going to learn to figure things out on my own.

Brock scheduled an appointment for the next day with a marriage counselor that specialized in betrayal recovery, sexual issues, and infidelity. I went with him to the appointment to humor his hope, absolutely convinced that any therapist worth their salt would hear my story and look at me with all sincerity and say, "Of course you should leave. He is a real piece of shit."

We met Dr. Lisa, and she was warm and welcoming. She was older than us, but not old. A tall, solid, middle-aged woman with kind eyes and a thin, firm mouth. She had multiple seating options in her spacious office, and I pointedly chose an arm chair instead of the couch. Brock sat in the armchair next to mine, but he couldn't touch me. That was the idea. I also didn't have to look at him as I briefly explained to Dr. Lisa why we were there; I wanted to divorce my lame husband, and he wanted me to stay. I gave her a quick and cutting overview of all of the dysfunction and laziness, the video games and the unemployment, the porn… and the pregnancy. I told her with utter certainty that I was sure I was leaving, and my presence at the session was just a formality. I just needed someone official to convince Brock that we were over.

Dr. Lisa listened to my rant quietly and compassionately. She nodded and paused thoughtfully as she formed her response in her mind. And because I was just so fucking angry, every word that came out of her mouth made me mad.

She told me that it was completely understandable that I wanted to leave, and she wouldn't blame me if I decided not to stay. She told me no one could fault me for leaving, and my feelings were valid.

But.

"But," she said, "I would ask you, if you are willing, to press pause. To pause the choice to leave, and give Brock some time to do some work. Rest assured, he has A LOT of work to do! And it's possible his work will make no difference. But if you can pause and give him a chance, you may find yourself changing your mind."

I.

Was.

So.

Mad.

She also gently reminded me that I wouldn't want to be alone forever, and that any potential future partner would have their own share of problems to work with—at least, in this scenario, I knew what my partner's issues were.

At the end of that visit, Brock agreed to see Dr Lisa for private therapy over the next several weeks, and I reluctantly agreed to pause, to give him time to do the work. Not because I thought it would be worth it, but because I had already committed to the idea that I wasn't coming back, and none of it mattered anyways.

We walked out of that therapy session like fire and ice. I was burning with rage, absolutely livid that she would suggest that our marriage could be healed. *OF COURSE SHE WOULD, she charges $250 per hour!* Brock was icy-cool, calm satisfaction. He believed that we were going to be okay, and I was going to stay.

I didn't. I packed up my two toddlers and flew alone to Hinton, Alberta, Canada. My mom and dad picked us up from the airport, and it was wonderful. I was safe, loved, and home. I didn't miss Brock, I didn't need him, and I didn't spare him a single thought. Everything was turning around. It was all finally going to be okay.

chapter 8

I had just spent nearly an entire year with Brock's parents, and found no help at all. Yet, somehow I had expected my mom and dad to be engaged and supportive, and to walk with me through the hardship that is parenting multiple small kids. I thought they would take some weight off of my shoulders. I thought they would support my parenting choices. I thought they would dig deep, meet me where I was, and finally someone, *anyone* would care a whole lot about me.

What I did NOT think was that they would fill my kids with crap (candy and cookies and ice cream) all day, every day. I did not think that they would be unable to say no to every whim and request. I did not think that they would buy every toy and stuffy and game that my children asked for. Let them skip naps. Leave the TV on, regardless of my requests. Take them to restaurants and then get huffy when they acted like toddlers. They *were* toddlers. I couldn't believe how bad it was. I just didn't truly believe things worked that way.

Under no circumstances, real or imagined, did I think I would miss Brock because he had quietly supported me in parenting our children in a loving and hugely unrecognized way. I left Charlotte thinking that I wasn't going to miss him because he was lazy, and useless. It wasn't until I was with my parents that I was able to see the truth... how functionally Brock actually helped me. How he helped calm everyone down when our children were loud and crazy. How he helped comfort them when they were sad. How he gave baths, and did bedtimes, and filled sippy cups, and got snacks, and picked out clothes. He talked to them and loved them and sang to them and kissed them and rough-housed with them when they were wild.

Oh my god, I realized on my second day in Canada, *Brock is actually a really, really good dad.*

So. Brock had been a wonderful dad all along, and I just hadn't allowed myself to see it. I had been too angry to notice what he *was* doing, and too focused on all the things he *wasn't* doing. I hadn't been fair to him because I wanted to be right. I felt so freaking bad all of the time, and I needed it to be his fault.

Knowing all of that, feeling it deep within me, didn't soften my heart nor my resolve. Even though I had become aware that Brock was more than I had given him credit for, I was still so angry at him for all of the hurt I was feeling. If nothing else, I had already decided that I would never stay because of the porn. I didn't want to give him another chance. In fact, I doubled down. I decided that, since I was getting divorced, and I was already pregnant and, since I had my parents to help with the kids, I was going to give myself full permission to do whatever I wanted.

I had never fucked around, and it was time for me to find out.

One evening, I went out to the bar with my oldest brother Adam, and his wife Sarah. We ordered drinks, (I got a coke—pregnant) and chatted. I hadn't told them of my newly made FAAFO plans, but I glanced around the bar trying to decide which fella I was going to pick-up for the night. While I didn't have the highest self-esteem in the universe, especially because I was starting to *feel* pregnant, I was aware that I was young, thin, and relatively attractive. I was pretty sure that I could find someone interested in spending time with me, even if I didn't really know what I wanted that time to look like. I also wasn't in a rush. I enjoyed my evening with my brother and his wife.

While we were chatting, I had briefly explained to him about the issue with porn in our marriage. I was utterly shocked when he bravely admitted that it had been a problem in his marriage as well. As with the infidelity between our parents, it hadn't really occurred to me that porn was a problem for anyone else, let alone with my own brother. I was absolutely astounded that he was willing to share that tender information with me, but more importantly, it *normalized* it. We weren't the only people in the world going through that particular hell. What a gift that was to know.

Adam and Sarah stayed with me for a few hours, but when they were ready to leave, I decided to get serious about interacting with other dudes. Strange men. Humans that I didn't know. Hands that had never touched me. Eyes that I didn't adore. Lips that didn't transfix me. As I walked through the bar and discreetly appraised potential partners, my eyes filled with tears and I came to understand that I actually didn't *want* any of them. I didn't want those hands, or that smile, or those eyes. It had taken weeks of separation, a trip across the continent, and a night in a noisy, crowded bar, but in that moment my heart finally softened.

I didn't want to kiss any of them.

The resolve that I had stubbornly built and refused to yield had shattered. With an unintentional sob, I turned on my heel and hurried out of the bar. I rushed back to my parents home, my chest filled with the ache of longing and the grief of leaving a relationship that I wasn't actually done with.

I still really, really loved Brock.

While the rest of his family was in Canada, Brock took a deep dive into the world of therapy and "doing the work." He saw Dr. Lisa multiple times per week, and dug into reasons that he was seeking porn, and not seeking a job. She asked him to do a life audit, and to identify all of the big-T trauma and little-t traumas he had experienced as far back as his memory went. Then he had to identify what stories and beliefs he had about himself because of those traumas. She also lovingly but firmly guided him to understand that porn was not actually a benign, one-way experience. It was hurting him, it was hurting his wife, and it was, in-fact, infidelity.

I wasn't aware of the depth and breadth of the work Brock was doing while I was busy falling back in love with him in Canada. About a week into our trip, I video-called him so he could speak to his children. He wept through the whole call, and even though my heart had changed, I maintained as much of my cool demeanor as I could manage. He told me that he had applied for and had an upcoming interview at a big tech firm in Mooresville just north of Charlotte, and he was hopeful. He told me that our renters had given their notice, and he was going to move us out of his parents house, and back into our townhome. He told me that he felt good, and strong, and worthy—and that he was doing those things whether or not I decided to come home. He was doing them for himself, not just to make me stay. Talking with him, I could feel that things had shifted. He felt different.

That night, after too much sugar, television and not enough outside time, I lost my temper at Ronan for some transgression, and grabbed him by the hand to pull him into a time-out. Ronan was so shocked by the suddenness of my action that he did the only thing he could think of to free himself, and he bit me. He pulled my hand that was holding his up to his mouth, and bit down hard. He wouldn't let go. I screamed out in pain, which I'm sure scared him even more, and then I did the only possible, logical thing my brain could think of—I slapped him across the face with my free hand. To make him let go. He did, and I sat there next to him, shocked and in shock, while he cried and stared at me in equal parts fear and confusion. In all, it took about 30 seconds from start to finish.

What the fuck just happened?

In the absolute opposite of anything resembling help, my mother immediately berated me for hitting my son, and my dad shouted that he had had enough. He was at the end of his rope with all of the noise and mess and constant too-much-ness of two toddlers in their tiny apartment. Feeling like a terrible mother and a terrible daughter at the same time, I came apart. I broke down in sobs of failure and desolation. And in that exact moment, it became abundantly clear that Ronan, Ruby and I could not stay with my parents any longer. We were not in the safe haven that I had hoped for; instead, we were in some strange, painful purgatory, and we had to leave. I texted Brock and told him that we would be coming home.

It was surprisingly refreshing to come home to *not Judy and Tim's house*. Brock had moved all of our things back into the townhome, and unpacked. He had also set up separate bedrooms for us, to honor the fact that we were still 'separated'. He didn't want to put any pressure on me to decide whether or not to stay married. That was so nice. It felt safe, and like he was taking me seriously. We then agreed, for the time being, to cohabitate and co-parent, and allow ourselves the space to work on our relationship without attachment to the outcome.

We started seeing Dr. Lisa together every week. I wasn't convinced that things would improve, nor that I would end up wanting to stay married, but I was more open to the possibility than I had been before my Canadian fiasco. Brock also shared his life audit with me, and I found myself moved deeply into compassion. There were so many wounds he had been walking around with that I had never known existed. It made some space within me to allow him to struggle. I found empathy and saw him with different eyes.

Around the same time, I informed Brock that I was planning a home birth for our third baby, and that he was welcome to attend if he were so inclined, but I wasn't willing to change my plans because of his comfort level. I braced myself for push-back, but he supported me whole-heartedly, and we walked through every stage of the process together.

Over the following months, we continued seeing Dr. Lisa, both separately and together. She was patient with us, and an absolute fountain of knowledge and wisdom. She taught us how to effectively communicate, and how to talk through things without 'winning'. She showed us how to hear each other without only trying to be heard. She explained the value of acting like adults in our relationships, rather than a whole host of other roles that we might fall into—martyr and child and parent and victim.

Far and away, though, the best advice I got from Dr. Lisa was when I saw her for a private session. We were talking about me, and my history, and where my own issues and stories were coming from.

"I'm just so lonely," I told her.

She nodded, and said that she thought that it was possible that I just needed to make friends with myself. That, if I enjoyed my own company, I wouldn't ever be alone.

That answer irritated me so much—*I just need to like myself?? That will fix everything??*—that I nearly stopped listening to what she had to say, and then I would have missed the magic.

We went on to talk about how I didn't know what to do—how to decide to stay married, or decide to leave. I felt like there was no possible way to know which choice was best, and I was so lost, so afraid of making a mistake. She asked me then if I'd had any regrets over what choices I made with my ex-husband, and how I handled that situation.

I thought about it for a few moments, before I slowly said, "No. I don't have any regrets." And I didn't. "I can't regret those choices because, looking back, I absolutely did the best I could with the knowledge I had at the time. Even if I know better now, back-then-Mandy couldn't know what I know." I looked directly at her as I pronounced, "I don't have any regrets at all."

She looked solidly back at me, unwavering, and said, "Don't you think it's possible that few-years-from-now-Mandy will look back at right-now-Mandy, and trust that whatever decision you make is the right one based on the information you have in THIS moment?"

My eyes immediately filled with tears. It blew my mind. I had never looked at it that way before; as though the person I would be in the future could possibly be kind to the person I was right then. Future me could be kind to present-day me. I took a deep breath, and realized she was right. I felt a soft sort of peace. The one where I knew I wasn't going to look back on these days and weeks and months, and wish I had done it all differently. Because

I was already doing the best I could, with the information I had. Future me would be kind to me. And that was a gift.

Over the next months of my unintended pregnancy, Brock and I cooked together, and cleaned together, and raised our children together; we *did not* sleep together. We interviewed and chose a homebirth midwife that I fell deeply in love with, and found myself excited to walk through the birthing journey once again. For the first time since discovering I was pregnant with Ronan, I felt some brightness coming to my life. The glimmers of a sunrise past the horizon, where joy might be. I was so grateful for Brock and what he contributed to our household, and also to his new job that seemed to fill him up with passion! And purpose! And worth! The future looked rosy, and I could see it. I could see it.

On a cold, blustery November morning, nearly two full weeks past my 'due' date, I finally felt the first twinges of labor. I, as of yet, had never gone into labor on my own, and I wasn't sure what it would feel like. Not wanting to sound the alarm too early, I went downstairs to the living room, bounced on a labor ball, and watched America's Funniest Home Videos. When it became clear to me that my contractions were getting stronger, and that I was progressing and not fizzling out, I let my midwife know.

Another quite predictable six hours later, Ryder Kane was in my arms in what was the most beautiful home birth I could have imagined, and I sobbed with joy. And Brock sobbed with joy. And oh my word, how could I have ever thought we didn't want him? He was here. And he was JOY.

In the sweet, quiet, lovingly peaceful hours after birthing my third child in my bathtub, I was tucked into my bed and fed a giant plate of turkey and stuffing and mashed potatoes. Ryder was born on Thanksgiving day, and would forever be known as our Thanksgiving baby. As my new baby and I wound down from the work of the day, and settled in for a well-earned nap, Brock crawled into bed across from me and we curled up around our newborn son. Our eyes met over the head of our boy, and we both gently wept. Ryder was here, and we were together, as though it was actually *was* always meant to be. I finally knew. Nothing needed to be said, and no decision needed to be made. Brock fell asleep in bed with us that night, and never left our bedroom again.

chapter 9

He was here, and he was magic. I spent hours and hours gazing lovingly into Ryder's eyes, and allowed myself to be filled up with the joy of his existence. My sweet squish. My sugah-boogah. My Wydah. I was so deeply in love with him, and so, so thankful he was born.

Every now and then, though, as I was staring at him, Ryder's eyes seemed to pierce deeply into my own soul and I would feel an overwhelming ache; an unfamiliar sadness. It was a deep sorrow and longing that surprised and worried me. It happened more than once, and it was undeniable. I started to tell Brock that I was concerned—I started to believe that Ryder was telling me he wasn't going to stay. A quiet apology, like he wanted me to be ready. It didn't surprise me. He was just too beautiful for this earth.

I wondered and fretted, and held him so tightly. I breathed him in so fully. I reveled and marveled in his existence, and tried to wish away the feeling that he wouldn't be here for long. I was on the look-out, constantly, for anything that might take him away from me. And Ryder, that magical third baby, gave me no shortage of hair-pulling false-alarms; from the time he choked on a scrabble tile and I called 911, to the time he squirted bleach into his mouth, to the day he rode his bike out into a busy road, and the oncoming car couldn't see him. Every time, my heart dropped into a pit and I was sure, "This is it. This is when I lose him."

Only, he didn't go.

Ryder grew beautifully, and matured, and brought joy to what were mostly dim days. Parenting still overwhelmed me. I still hadn't reconciled what being a mother to small children truly was. It was supposed to be beautiful and idyllic, and my children were supposed to love me, and I wasn't supposed to just be getting snacks and wiping asses all day. My house was a literal disaster—food stains on the carpet and a trash pile of a couch, laundry in every nook and cranny. Sticky… Everything.

Finally, years into a struggle that wouldn't let up, I realized that I might actually be suffering from clinical depression. I don't know why it took me so long to consider it, but once I saw it, I couldn't unsee it. I pondered it for a few days, but eventually I decided to talk to someone. I knew that life wasn't so dark for other people, and although there were flashes of the most brilliant magic moments, the sparks were so obscured that I could hardly see them through the fog.

It all came to a head one afternoon when things were the worst they'd ever been. We were driving home from preschool, and Ryder was screaming in the car seat. Ruby was yelling because Ryder was yelling, and I was shouting at Ronan to try to give him back his pacifier. Ronan was stressed out, and couldn't reach the pacifier, and started crying because I was yelling at him. I was sweating, and anxious, and angry, and suddenly I thought, *All it would take is to swerve my car into the other lane.* It would be so fast. We wouldn't suffer. It would just be so easy to end everything; the pain, the mess, the exhaustion. The intensity of that thought—and the fact that it felt so rational—scared the shit out of me.

I had that thought, and then I couldn't get level. I couldn't breathe back into my body, I couldn't put the kids in front of the TV to take a second, I couldn't escape the chaos inside my mind. I didn't even unbuckle them from the car. I was feeling so dark, and everything there felt so scary. I was afraid of myself.

I texted Brock at work, and told him I needed him to meet me for lunch. He didn't ask any questions. He just said, "I can be there in 15 minutes."

I dropped our three small children off at a local drop-in daycare, where they were well known and well loved, and drove to our usual lunch place. Brock was already there and had already ordered our food. He was sitting outside in the full sun, because he knew me. He looked up at me with sad, scared eyes, the depth of his concern written all over his face. He could clearly see that I was not okay. I was crying before I even sat down.

"Something has to change," I told him bleakly. "I don't think I can keep going. I'm dangerous, Brock. I'm hurting our kids. I yell too much and I hit too much, and I'm just so fucking mad all the time, even though they are so good."

Brock listened, and chewed on his nails, "I believe you, babe. I know it's hard. I don't know how to help. I don't know what else to do." He reached over and put his hand on top of mine.

"I think I need to be hospitalized, Brock," I sobbed, "I thought about crashing the car today. Killing all of us. I'm just so fucking scared."

It was the hardest truth I'd ever spoken, and no one knew how bad it was—no one was in my head. No one was home alone with me all day. No one saw. Not even Brock.

I was so broken. I so desperately wanted my life to be what I had dreamed of—and truly, I had everything that I had ever dreamed of having—and it was all so loud and awful and terrible. I was ashamed that it was hard for me. I was ashamed that I didn't love being a mother. I was ashamed because, truly, I mostly hated it.

We talked through what in-patient hospitalization could look like, and what we would have to do with the kids; who could help us, what support we had, what our options were for work and money and childcare and time. Almost right away, we realized that our biggest fear was that someone would take our kids away because I was absolutely bat-shit crazy, and they would never give them back. Or that if I went in somewhere, they wouldn't let me out. It was all too big and scary to even look directly at, even if none of those things were actually true.

I started crying harder. There was no good option. No life-line. No lamp in the darkness. I couldn't even find a flashlight.

We sat there, silent and deeply concerned, fearful for the future, when Brock finally squeezed my hand and asked, "What about meds, Mand? What about anti-depressants? What if they could help??"

I immediately shook my head, no. I couldn't. There was so much stigma and judgment attached to needing to be medicated. I had been so thoroughly clean and crunchy, an 'organic-granola' mother to my kids. I didn't want to need them. Drugs felt like failing.

Brock leaned forward, and put his face as close to mine as he could. He rested his forehead gently on my brow, as he had in Arkansas. He closed his eyes, and said, ever so quietly, "I know you don't want to need them, babe. But what if… what if they aren't something that you need forever? Like… what if you are under water and you can't swim? You can totally take swimming lessons. Or we can get you a life jacket. Or you can decide not to swim anymore. But first, absolutely first, we have to get you out of the water."

He opened his eyes, and looked at me, one hand on each shoulder. "The meds wouldn't be forever, babe. They are just to get you out of the water."

My eyes filled with tears. I knew that what he was saying was absolute truth. I was drowning. My whole entire life was just far too much for me, and I needed help. And I knew, as I had learned at 6 years old staring up at the surface: there was no way to learn to swim while standing on the bottom.

"Let's get you out of the water."

So I did it. I fearfully but bravely opened up to my doctor, and began on a low dose of Zoloft. And quite literally, almost overnight, light exploded in my life in resplendent glory. Like a beam of sunshine through a prism, I saw beauty and magic everywhere I looked. I had patience and peace. I was kind and gentle. The constant ebb of anger and resentment finally flowed away from me. The tasks of motherhood and the burden of keeping my home no longer overwhelmed me. The change was almost immediate, and it was undeniable. I was functional, joyful, and calm within my own life, the way I'd always wanted.

It was glorious. And it would not last long.

When Ryder was nearly two years old, I was sitting on the couch after we had put all the kids to bed. I glanced around the tidy living room, dishes done and dinner put-up, and looked at Brock and speculatively, my single eyebrow raised.

"What?" he asked.

"I dunno," I hedged, trying to put my thoughts into words. "I was just thinking. Like… Do you want any more kids? Do you feel like you're finished? Is three enough?"

We had worked so long and hard on our relationship. Two years later, and we'd found our way through arguments and fights, and learned how to communicate honestly, vulnerably. We'd practiced validating each other and echoing back what we'd heard rather than defending or problem solving. We'd toiled long and hard on recovering trust and reclaiming safety in the bedroom in our post-pornography era. It wasn't always easy—in fact it rarely was—but we were seeing the fruits of those labors. We were closer and more in love than we'd ever been before.

Brock's gaze zoomed out as he looked away, and responded, "I'm pretty happy, you seem pretty happy… I love our kids. Life feels good. I think three is plenty." He nodded slowly, as he turned to meet my eyes. "Yeah… I'd say I'm done."

Maybe I was hormonal, maybe I was emotional, or maybe it was a trick question, but I immediately burst into tears and exclaimed with level 100 intensity, "How can you just be done?! Just like that? You don't ever want to have any other babies? None?? Brock, seriously. I cannot. There is no way I could say that I was just done like that."

Solidly nine years into relationship with me, with hours and hours of therapy under his belt, Brock knew what was happening, and he chuckled as he said, "I'm not saying it's not still open for discussion, Mandy! We can always talk about it." He leaned forward and kissed me gently on the lips. "We will always keep talking about it."

Almost instantly mollified, I grinned and replied, "Well. That's good. But just in case, if you don't want to have another baby, we really shouldn't have sex tonight… I'm ovulating."

I guess as soon as he saw my smile, he tuned back into the television, and despite my caution, I must assume what he heard was, "Whomp whomp whomp whomp whomp whomp whomp… sex tonight."

Because two weeks later, I was pregnant with our fourth child. As soon as I realized I was pregnant, I stopped taking the Zoloft. I was minimally comfortable taking meds while breastfeeding, but highly anxious about medicating myself while pregnant. I had hoped that some of the routines and habits I'd put in place while on the anti-depressants would keep me from sinking back down into the dark place, and mostly they did.

Ryder, as sweet and wonderful and delightful as he was, had been plagued with early tooth decay. From the moment his front top teeth erupted, they had begun to crumble and discolor. We spent several years trying to hold off the inevitable, but eventually it became gravely apparent that he'd need to have several of his teeth pulled, and the remaining teeth crowned with stainless steel caps. He was only 2 years and a few months old when he was scheduled to undergo general anesthesia at a hospital for the extensive dental procedure.

I crawled into bed beside him the night before his surgery, and I held him next to me as I cried and cried and cried. I had never forgotten the message that his eyes had poured into me as a newborn, and I was sure *this was it*. I just knew I was going to lose him, and I was absolutely not okay.

After hours of fretting and weeping, I finally cried myself into sleep, and immediately awoke into the nightmare that I had been dreading. Ryder was next to me, and his body was cold. He was already gone. I was not aware that I was dreaming, and I started screaming—something had taken him in the night. In the wildly, vividly real dream, I keened as I held his dead body, and then, in the fashion of dreams, I lived through the next several weeks. The funeral. The grief. The crying and the pain. The devastation.

I gasped awake, suddenly, urgently and Ryder was next to me—warm and sweaty and healthy and well. So vital and so vibrant, it took my breath away. I sobbed anew and gathered him into my arms again with the relief and joy that he was just fine, but the message was clear. It was so abundantly clear, and I could feel it with every fiber of my being—*he is here, and he is real, and when it is his time, there is nothing you can do to change it or wish it away or prevent it.* I didn't know for sure where the message came from. I had no specific religion or belief. Despite not knowing where from, I knew it was true. I knew it. He could die in the car on the way to the surgery. He could die from an infection because of the surgery. He could die from a fever in the middle of the night while he slept. "You are not in control."

You are not in control.

I am not in control.

I was completely overcome with the deepest and most surreal peace in that moment. He was going to be okay, or he was going to die, and it didn't matter what I did or how I acted or felt, because I wasn't in control. There was nothing that I could do to change it; all I could do was face it with bravery, and trust that no matter what happened, *I* would survive.

I would have to.

We went on to the surgery, and it was all hard. It was hard to trust, and hard to watch happen, and so hard to see him suffer coming out of anesthesia—but he did not die. In the days following, he did not struggle nor falter. The procedure was nothing but good. He was okay, and I was okay, and everything was okay.

The rest of my fourth pregnancy progressed uneventfully. It wasn't bright-shiny-beautiful all the time, but it wasn't dark-gloomy-dangerous either. As we inched closer and closer to delivery, I began to wonder if we had made a massive mistake. We were so complete, the five of us. Life was really good. Was having a fourth child going to ruin everything? Would there be room? What was I even doing?

When labor began, all of the fears fell away in the face of the work. I had hired the same midwife to be with us for my second home birth, and I was safe and supported. I fully expected a repeat of my prior experiences; six hours of labor, and a few powerful pushes. Only, the hours went on and on. Eight, and then ten, and then more. The baby wasn't coming. I didn't understand what was happening, I didn't know what was wrong, and I was angry about that too. *This was supposed to be easy. I was supposed to be good at this by now. This baby should have come out already.*

Brock held me as I cried out all my frustrations between contractions. I was so angry. I just wanted it to be over already. I wanted to hold my baby. I knew the hardest part, that complete surrender was still ahead of me. It was taking so fucking long, and I was just so mad. Suddenly, in a flash of insight, I realized that my birth wasn't what it was supposed to be—it couldn't be that. It could only be what it was. The birth was *what it was.* And my fighting it with anger and disappointment and supposed-to-bes was just making me suffer.

Birth doesn't conform to *supposed to be's.* It doesn't care what we think or want or hope for. Birth is what it is.

The birth I was experiencing wasn't the problem—it was my *expectation* of what I wanted that birth to be. With that realization, I surrendered in my heart to the reality of the birth that I was walking through, as it was, and just let it be. Complete acceptance.

Finally it was time to push. Time to dig deep, and find the scary place that meant the baby was coming out. The surrender of the body. Only, this birth wasn't just different in that it was so much longer—but also, that the scary place was so much deeper, and so much blacker than it had ever been before. When it was time to push, I went completely away. Within the confines of my own mind, I went entirely into a pit of darkness and found myself enveloped in terror. Deep, penetrating fear, unlike anything I had ever known before. It was agony. It wasn't the physical birth of the baby (he came out just like all the others had in a few strong pushes) but, it was that *I wasn't there*. I was far, far away, sunk deep into the immensity of that black hole inside myself. I was lost.

Someone had to tell me, "Mandy, open your eyes! The baby is out!" I was still thrashing in fear and pain when I forced my eyes open, and there he was. Glory. Our fourth beautiful baby, another boy, a perfect, sweet, tiny Rory Kai.

The sparkle and the magic and the glitter, it all came pouring back. In a rush, a fraction of an instant of a moment, Rory was born and we were, all of us, surrounded in blazing, blinding light.

chapter 10

Rory!

Oh Rory. Our newest, little love. He was everyone's baby. And we delighted in him.

I settled easily into the beautiful early days of postpartum, and we took life slowly. We watched so much Paw Patrol, and we ate so many snacks, and we loved the moment when Dada got home every evening. I took the big kids to the pool and supervised them as they paddled around in the shallow end while I sat and nursed my delicious little brown baby in the shade. Ronan and Ruby were blonde haired, blue-eyed cherubs. Ryder had brown hair and brown eyes and tanned like the dickens. Rory took it to extremes; you couldn't see his pupils for the darkness of his eyes, and his skin was the warmest, creamy brown. We had decided within hours of his birth that Rory was our last, and we reveled in all of the "last firsts"—this time, not wishing any of it away nor rushing any moment. The last first smile. The last first laugh. The last baby blues.

I was deliriously happy while I was in newborn heaven, but that stage cannot and does not last. As we moved through Rory's infancy, and adjusted to sending Ronan to Kindergarten, I knew I was skating the fine line between being in the light and falling into darkness. I was doing everything I knew to do, and leaning into all of the self-care rituals I had learned while on medication: meditation, eating and drinking enough, deep breathing practices, and prioritizing rest. Sometimes it was enough. Sometimes, nothing was enough.

Unless one has a child like Ryder, it's hard to believe that the stories are not exaggerated. Let me assure you, they are the complete and utter truth. Magic little Thanksgiving baby grew into a toddler that knew his power, and was inexhaustibly determined to show it to the world. And to me. Over and over.

Not a single day went by that didn't find our Ryder entangled in some sort of hair-raising, teeth-gnashing endeavor. Perhaps he was dumping a paint can on the carpet, and walking through it. Maybe he was throwing all of the books off of the bookshelves, and ripping out the pages. It's entirely possible he was gleefully jumping around in a basket of freshly folded laundry. There once was a bucket of fireplace ashes. So. Many. Markers.

If it was quiet, he was not peacefully playing somewhere; if it was quiet, there was immediate cause for concern.

Because of my healing journey, I had been on the path to a more peaceful, respectful parenting. I had been learning that I wanted to be calm instead of reactive. I was figuring out that my rages and triggers were mine, and really had nothing to do with my children—that it was my responsibility to figure out what they were, and to diffuse them. The thing about a kid like Ryder is that he doesn't just figure out what buttons to push, he pushes all of them. He mashes on them relentlessly. He can't help it.

I snapped early one morning when, upon coming down the stairs for the first time, I found that Ryder had been up before me and had used a black ballpoint pen all over the cushion of my brand-new cream and oak glider. The one that I had allowed myself to purchase as a gift and reward for safely birthing our fourth child, and wishing for a beautiful, comfortable place to sit and rock him to sleep. Scribbles. Black and deep. Everywhere.

I saw red.

All of my newly practiced and tenuous self control, all of my razor-thin patience shattered in an instant, and I utterly raged on my three year old. I shouted, and I belittled, and I demeaned. I told him that I hated him. And I picked up his prized red lego car, his beloved birthday present, and held it in front of his face as

I said, "You ruin my stuff, I ruin yours." I shattered it into pieces while he watched.

Even as I was losing my temper and blowing up at my sweet, challenging son, I knew it was wrong. I knew that it wasn't how I wanted to act, or how I wanted to treat him, and most certainly not how I wanted him to feel. I broke my own heart while I was breaking his.

No sooner was the lego spread all across the floor than I was scooping him up into my arms, and apologizing. *Oh Ryder. I'm so sorry. Bud, I'm so sorry. I shouldn't have done that. I should never have done that. I don't hate you. I could never hate you. I'm sorry I'm sorry I'm sorry.*

It was wrong. And I know you hate me right now. I hate me too. It was the event that convinced me that it was beyond time for something to shift, and abundantly clear that it had to come before I caused more pain. Brock and I spoke frankly about going back on antidepressants, and I offered a new avenue I hadn't tried before. *What if,* I wondered, *what if I just try therapy for a while? Let me try that first, and see what happens.*

I started seeing a new therapist the following week, and she was a breath of fresh air. For the first six months, I saw her twice a week. I was desperate to make progress and preserve my relationships with my husband, my kids, myself.

Abbie was kind and soft spoken. She heard me completely, and she never disagreed. She would nod, and validate my feelings, and then she would ask if she could offer me a new perspective. "What if," she would ask, "what if you looked at it this way instead?"

Very, very slowly, I started to see myself in a kinder, gentler light. I started to have a clearer perception about what my role was as mother, and what I didn't have to allow in my home. I stopped viewing some of the realities of motherhood as me failing; the house was messy, yes, but it was meant to be. The kids were wild, yes, but they were meant to be. It was hard, she told me, but it was never, ever meant to be easy. Abbie gave me permission to put myself first, and to see that the benefits of that would roll downhill, improving life for everyone. The switch wasn't flipped overnight, but I slowly felt myself stepping out of the shadows, and there was steady progress towards being the mama that I had always wanted to be, the mama I had dreamed of.

In a way that I could never have predicted, not expecting life to be perfect—allowing it to be chaotic—somehow caused it to be less challenging. I was much more able to go with the flow. It wasn't actually any different, I just didn't struggle so badly with it.

One afternoon, after taking a bath with Rory, I stood in front of the mirror, and silently berated myself for my squishy, round, postpartum body. I had gained more weight with Rory's pregnancy then I had any of the others, and I was terrible to myself about it. I had not ever noticed before how mean my internal voice was, but the dark and angry thoughts were swirling around in my brain. I didn't want to be the size that I was, and I couldn't figure out how to be okay.

In a sudden flash of insight, holding my beautiful baby that I loved unconditionally, I realized, "*You know… I have hated myself and my body for the last thirty-three years, and have not yet been able to hate myself into someone I love. What if I tried loving myself instead?*" My eyes filled with tears at the thought. What if I loved myself instead?

That day, I began what turned into a life-long journey towards radical self-love and acceptance. It started with saying nice things to myself every time I looked in the mirror, and grew into a practice of being gentle with my own mistakes, and forgiving myself for failing. I became better at stopping myself from falling completely into a shame spiral, and would instead recognize what was happening, and call it into the light It was tiny progress, little by little, but one minuscule rung at a time, I built a ladder for myself out of the chasm of darkness.

The week before Christmas, Brock was scheduled to have a vasectomy. Rory was six months old, and still wonderful. Every moment being his mother was a gift. But that fourth birth was *not* my favorite, and because of it, I didn't want to have any more children. Brock already asked me, 'Please don't ever make me watch you go through that again," and we knew we were both done.

The night before his procedure, we were standing together in the kitchen, talking about what the next day would look like and my gut suddenly clenched in fear. "I don't think I want you to go through with it," I told him. I wasn't sure why I felt that way, but my intuition was usually spot on, and I had learned to lean into it.

"What? Why not?", he asked. I was the one that had pushed for the big V, and we both agreed it was the best possible option amongst a list of not great options for birth control.

"I don't really know. I just… feel not okay." I couldn't explain what was going on with me. I had no words to describe what I was experiencing. All I knew was that my intuition was rarely wrong, and my gut was screaming at me.

"It's going to be fine, love," he assured me, "It's simple. Nothing is going to happen. No big deal."

"I know," I exclaimed, and couldn't stop the tears from filling my eyes. "It's not that. It's just… so permanent. Like, we can never have any other kids? Forever. What if we change our minds? What if… Brock…" I gulped, and then sobbed out, "…*what if one of our kids dies?*"

He folded me in his arms and held me tightly against him, "Oh babe. That's not going to happen. That's not going to happen!" He didn't let me go, and we stood there, swaying gently back and forth in the kitchen as my tears freely flowed.

"If we ever decide that we want more kids, or something terrible happens, we can always get it reversed. We always have that option." He stroked my hair, and his reassurances calmed my fears.

The next day, we went through with the snip. It was quick, and relatively easy, and his recovery was smooth.

It also did wonderful things for our sex life. Not worrying about getting pregnant is a pretty powerful aphrodisiac.

As time went on, and everyone got older, and therapy helped more and more, I started finding myself in the light more often than not. Instead of most of the time in the shadow of depression, with brief sparks of glory, I was happy to be mostly shiny with a few grim excursions into gloom. But those moments didn't last. I didn't stay in the dark. I was doing yoga, and treating myself to acupuncture, and reading a load of books that did me a world of good. Eckhart Tolle and Brené Brown and Glennon Doyle. *The Seven Spiritual Laws of Yoga*, and *Siddartha*, and *Dying to be Me*. Books about life, and books about pain, and books about presence. It was all working.

One of the things that I had come to recognize in therapy was that I had always dreamed of being a mother—but since that dream had come true, and I was a mother, I had no new dream. It wasn't as though my life had stopped—there was still so much living to do. I needed a goal, something to look forward to. I loved my job as an Ultrasound tech, but it wasn't my ultimate. There had to be more.

It didn't take me long to figure out that my births at home were so powerful and so transformational for me that I wanted more women to have access to care like that. I wanted more women to know themselves, and to see themselves and be seen as whole. I wanted their autonomy to be paramount. I wanted their choices and decisions to be turned around and handed back to them. I wanted them to be trusted so deeply that they could do nothing less than learn to trust themselves completely. And while it felt so huge, and improbable, and so far away—not quite like an impossible dream, but nearly so—I started quietly walking in that direction. I signed up for a Midwife Assistant training program, reached out to my midwife and told her I was interested in becoming her assistant, and for the first time in my adult life, I let myself dream big again.

Through time in therapy, sometimes together, and sometimes separately, Brock and I had identified that his parents were a sticking point in our relationship. They were, unintentionally I believe,

continuing to be harmful and cause contention in our home: arguments with his brothers, and his parents picking sides; being invited
over to go through old closets to find that they had gotten rid of
or given away treasured items; issues with belittling or making
fun of our kids for their idiosyncrasies and behaviors. More than
a few times, words were said that cut my husband's tender heart
so deeply, and it was just so painful. Time and time again, we
would have to talk through and figure out and decompress from a
thoughtless or demeaning interaction with one or both of them,
and it was exhausting. We just couldn't do anything right, and we
just couldn't do it any more.

With Abbie's guidance, we realized that it might be time to
put up some firmer boundaries, and maybe not give them quite so
much access to our lives and our hearts. We talked for days and days
about what those boundaries might have to look like, and came to
no easy decision. However, the attic above Judy and Tim's garage
had stored most of our items while we had lived with them, and a
large amount of it was left behind in Brock's hasty move. They had
asked us to come and get our stuff so they could do a decluttering
and deep clean of the garage. Brock and I agreed to go, and also
finally, reluctantly agreed that *cleaning day* would be the turning
point from which we would begin behaving differently. We would
go over to their home, and remove our things from the garage, and
then we were going to go no contact.

chapter 11

It was Saturday. Cleaning day. A cold, blustery February morning. I was laying in bed, slowly waking and nursing Rory and I remembered that Brock had said we were going to his parents house. I didn't want to get up. I thought about telling Brock to take the big kids, and that Rory and I would stay home. I thought about saying I was sick. I just didn't want to go.

The kids were excited. They loved their grandparents and loved going up to the lake. I dressed Rory in warm clothes, deliberately choosing articles that were Christmas gifts from Brock's mom.

The loose plan was to go through the attic above Judy and Tim's garage, to find all of the stuff that was ours and get rid of it. Take it, throw it, donate it—whatever. It had been three years since Brock had moved us out, and it was time. I was of the mindset to just throw everything away; we hadn't needed or used any of it in that time, I figured we could survive without it. Brock wanted to sort and keep everything. Judy just wanted help.

We arrived around ten, the kids spilling out of the car and barreling into the house. Brock, Judy, Tim and I stood around and chatted for a while, but it didn't take us long to decide to get to business. We had the kids come up into the attic with us to pick out a few vintage toys to play with, then sent them down to play in the garage below while we worked. The attic was full. Full full. *Oh fuck* full. Years and years of memorabilia, memories, and the detritus of a long life with three boys.

Without knowing what else to do, we got started opening

boxes and choosing things to throw or donate. In just a few hours we made a huge dent in the mess. There were several boxes in the back of my car to bring home, several more in the back of Judy's to go to donation, and absolutely tons in the trash pile. The kids had gotten bored with their chosen toys, and we were all cold and hungry, so we decided to go into the house to eat.

I sat and nursed Rory in the sun-room while everyone else prepared food. Rory was obviously sleepy, and I asked Brock if he would try to put him down for a nap—Rory only went down easily for Brock. They went downstairs into a bedroom together, I fed the kids, then sat down to eat my own lunch, and Brock was back upstairs before I had taken my first bite. Rory was so tired, he went down without hassle.

I guess we all sort of felt like we had worked hard enough for long enough that morning because we let lunch run long. We sat around talking while the big kids played in the living room, and then Uncle Brady arrived. I wasn't even aware he was coming, but everyone loved Uncle Brady, and his energy was a welcome addition. He ate lunch while we all caught up and chatted. It was nearly two when Judy and Brock headed outside to get back to work, bringing Brady with them. I stayed in the house with the kids, and waited for Rory to wake up. After a few minutes of playing on my phone, I went downstairs to check on him; it had been a long nap. His eyes popped open the minute I walked into the room, and he smiled at me. I was so happy to see him. We cuddled in the bed for a bit, and then he was ready to go. I asked if he wanted something to eat, and he nodded.

Nineteen month old Rory and I climbed up the stairs, and I got him a bun with some of the barbecued pork we'd had for lunch. He loved the bun, but did NOT love the barbecued pork—he took a bite and then immediately pulled it out of his mouth, and gingerly set it back down on the plate. I laughed at him and let him just eat the bun. We went outside where the other kids had migrated— there was a giant, flat parking area in front of the garage and a steep hill that rode down into it. Ronan and Ruby were playing with ancient action figures on the flat part of the driveway, and Ryder had taken a 'big-wheel' out of the garage and was freewheeling down the hill over and over again. Judy and Tim's big German short-haired Pointer, Max, was running happily around with the kids.

I stood in a patch of sunlight trying to keep warm and watched Rory walk into the garage to find something to play with. The guilt that Brock and Judy were up in the attic working, and I was just down in the driveway *doing nothing* churned like a fire in my belly. I watched as Brady carried a few loads of trash up to the trash pile at the top of the hill and watched as Tim loaded several more boxes into Judy's truck. I took videos of Ryder as came speeding down the hill, face filled with joy. Rory had found a little green tractor ride-on toy that he was pushing around like a lawn mower, proud of his treasure. Since everyone was sufficiently occupied, and the guilt had become oppressive, I climbed back up into the attic to check on Brock and Judy.

As I mounted the steps, I heard the crash of Rory's tractor slamming into the dog crate, and smiled as he giggled at the noise.

Crash. Giggle. Crash. Giggle. CRASH. Giggle.

I returned to the box I had been looking through before lunch and found some of Ronan's baby pictures and a few CD's that I wanted to keep. I was separating things into two different boxes— keep and throw. I paused mid-sort when I realized that I hadn't heard any crashing noises from the bottom of the stairs for a while. I didn't know for how long.

"I should go check on the kids," I said.

"They're fine," Brock told me. "I hear them outside this window." He pointed over his shoulder, and continued working. I glanced through another handful of discs, but something started to feel heavy. "I don't hear the kids," I said again, "I need to go check."

"My dad is down there," Brock told me, "and Brady."

"I know," I said, "But I'm just going to make sure."

I went down into the garage, expecting to see the kids playing quietly in the drive, but no one was there. The front door to the house was wide open, which was odd because it was very cold that day. *They must be inside. They left it open as they went inside.* I ran into the house and paused just inside the doorway, hoping to hear the kids, and felt a little thrill of fear.

Silence.

I jogged into the kitchen, and Tim was standing next to the counter on his phone. "You seen the kids?" I asked him. He shook his head no. I immediately turned and ran to the top of the stairs to the basement. "RONAN?" I shouted, "BRADY??" I listened for just a moment and didn't hear any response. My fear was rising, my chest tightening and my breath coming in shorter and shorter bursts.

I ran back out the front door and shouted up at the garage, "I CAN'T FIND THE KIDS!"

I heard Judy and Brock rush down the stairs. I started down the path to the water. When you live on the lake, you check the water. I found Rory's tractor abandoned off the path halfway to the backyard.

It's maybe 20 quick paces from the end of the pathway down to the edge of the lake. I ran it on stiff legs, and felt every step jolt up into my brain. I was cold and terrified.

Surely not. Surely not.

I felt almost separate from the event. It was so quiet, peaceful. Surreal. Beautiful. The water was smooth like glass, and reflected the sky perfectly. I stumped quickly down to the boat ramp and looked out across the water and it was perfectly smooth, except for a small break in the surface just off to the right of me.

It could be a stick. Let it be a stick.

But I couldn't see clearly in the mirrored sky, so I stepped up onto the boardwalk to get a better look.

Surely not.

Two steps up to my right from the boat ramp onto the boardwalk, I turned back to the water. I saw him. I saw his face looking towards me, still.

Unmoving.

No.

I screamed. And screamed. And screamed. Guttural. Deep. I screamed over and over and over. A separate part of my brain asked me why I was screaming like that—*wouldn't 'help' be better? Call 911?* Instead, I screamed.

That separate part of my brain was crystal clear, and completely aware of everything.

The water is not deep. You will not need to swim. Do not strip, just jump in. Throw your phone, you will need it later. Go.

I threw my phone out of my pocket and jumped down into the water, still screaming, that was ice-cold up to my thighs, then my waist. Three or four steps forward and I reached and pulled Rory up out of the water. He was limp and cold, his head rolled back in my arms. I screamed again. And again. As I walked, waterlogged, back towards the boat ramp, I started tipping him upside down and squeezing him to get the water out. *I need to get the water out to do CPR.* Water and vomit came pouring out. I screamed and screamed.

Faintly I heard Brock yell, *"CALL 911!! CALL 911!"* I glanced up where he was yelling and saw him jump off of the second story balcony of the house and tear his way down to us. As I stepped up onto the boardwalk again, I felt Brock beside me and that separate part of me marveled that he'd made it so quickly. I was still tipping Rory's body, and felt Brock pulling his cold, wet clothes off. I laid Rory down on the boardwalk, and began CPR. I didn't have to think about what to do—I had been trained and recertified every year for years.

Head tilt, chin lift. Open the airway. Breathe. Breathe.

I heard it gurgle in his lungs, and watched his chest rise.

It's going in. Compressions. Do compressions now.

I started compressing his chest. I counted, because that's what you do. I compressed and counted and then gave breaths again. His head was rolling around, and when I did compressions, vomit came out. I kept clearing the vomit and then resetting his head to do more breaths.

I heard Brock yelling, "GO BACK IN THE HOUSE. GO BACK INSIDE!" And I heard Ruby screaming in fear. I could not look. I could not stop. I couldn't. *Compressions and breaths. Compressions and breaths.* My entire world, all of existence was compressions and breaths.

Judy was hysterical on the phone next to me, and the 911 operator was instructing Judy how to tell me to do CPR. I paused long enough to shout, "I KNOW WHAT I'M DOING. STOP TALKING TO ME."

Suddenly, there was a body beside me. "Let me help," a voice said quietly. He did compressions to my breaths, pale hands emerging from a dark navy sweater. I did not look up, and never saw his face. *Move his blood. Breathe his lungs. Move his blood. Breathe his lungs.* There was no rational thought. Just breaths and counting and moving his blood and pushing his oxygen. I heard the sirens, and then the paramedics were there.

My partner moved away and someone else took over compressions. I continued to give breaths, hovering over my baby's frozen face, holding his head steady with his airway open. Finally, someone tapped my shoulder. They had equipment ready, and wanted to intubate him. I fell away... and howled.

I stopped doing CPR and suddenly my baby was there, in front of me, with no heartbeat, eyes open, not breathing and not crying, and I was screaming. Wailing. Keening. The sound of it came from the depths of me, and I couldn't stop. I couldn't make it quiet. I kept telling myself, *This isn't helping, Mandy. It's not helping them,* but I couldn't make it stop. Brock was holding on to me for dear life, calling, "My boy. My baby. Save my boy, please. My baby."

I started shivering uncontrollably as adrenaline wore off and I realized I was soaking wet. The medics had placed a breathing tube and continued compressions while they prepared Rory to go to the hospital. Someone asked if I wanted to ride in the ambulance. *Yes.* By then, the police had arrived and I heard them asking everyone what had happened. There was crime scene tape.

Judy brought me, shaking, into the house. I stripped my clothes off inside the doorway, pants and shoes, and we went upstairs to find dry clothes. I didn't speak. I didn't know what to say. We walked out to the ambulance, and I realized they hadn't made it up from the lake yet. It was a long, treacherous walk with a stretcher, and it was taking them time. They had to continue CPR as they walked. The ambulance driver pulled me into the cab of the ambulance and turned on the heat, full blast. He said something kind, and I don't remember what it was. He held my hand.

Brock came to the window of the cab and kissed me. I felt numb. I had stopped crying and wailing. I kept telling myself, "*That doesn't help. Just be here. Feel your feet on the ground. Just be here.*" They loaded Rory and the paramedics into the truck, and Brock said he would meet me at the hospital.

It took the driver of the ambulance three tries to turn the big rig around in the narrow drive, and then lights and sirens were on, and we were headed to the hospital, exactly 12 minutes away.

We arrived into the ER bay, and Rory was whisked away. A team was waiting for him, and I was moved off into a side room, offered warm blankets and water. I started shaking again. An officer came and sat next to me and said she wanted to take my statement. I didn't know what to do. Just before the ambulance drove off, Brock had said, "If the police question you, don't talk to anyone unless there is a lawyer present." I told her that.

The cop looked at me sideways, and said nastily, "Well, that just makes you look guilty."

I started sobbing and told her exactly everything that had happened. My son was in the next room, physically dead with hope falling away, and she forced me to 'give my statement'. Brock and his parents showed up while I was talking, and Brock was immediately angry. "This is not the time for this!" he shouted. Another other officer took him out into the hallway to calm him down. I finished speaking, feeling fully ravaged, and we sat in silence, waiting for news about Rory.

A few moments later, an ER doctor came in and gently introduced himself to us. He looked kind, but visibly shaken. He said he was in charge of Rory's care, and they were going to do everything they could. He turned to walk back out and stopped. Over his shoulder, he said to us, "I have kids too. I'm going to do *everything*."

We waited minutes that felt like an eternity. I don't know how many passed. Five? Fifteen? Fifty? When, finally, that same doctor burst back into the room and triumphantly shouted, "WE HAVE A HEARTBEAT!"

chapter 12

I screamed with relief. I was so prepared for him to be gone. I *knew* he was gone, and I had been telling myself to be ready for the news that he was gone. For the pain and the apology. The heartbeat... I screamed.

The doctor immediately calmed, and with tears in his eyes told us Rory had a heartbeat, but it still didn't look good. We didn't know how long he had been under for, and he'd had over 40 minutes of CPR. His heartbeat was slow, and they had called the life-flight team... but his heart rate had to maintain on its own above 60 beats per minute for them to fly him. They couldn't do CPR on the helicopter ride.

Then they allowed us to see him. He was on a high stretcher, surrounded by the accoutrements of medicine. An IV line in his shin, a tube down his throat. Someone was breathing for him, squeezing the bag, and I felt like *I should be doing that*. I wanted them to let me breathe for him. I watched his heart on the monitor as I touched him, held his hands and stroked his face. He was so cold. His little body was so cold. He didn't feel alive, but his heart was beating. I kissed his forehead and whispered to him. I told him to keep his heart beating so he could heal. I said I was sorry. So sorry.

The life-flight crew arrived as Rory's heart beat miraculously rose to 80 and then 100 on its own. The flight-paramedic checked his tubes and IVs, and said he would be safe to fly. They asked if I wanted to ride with them and I said yes. Yes was the only option.

Everyone else would drive. I took his amber necklace off, then, before we strapped him down to fly, and slipped it into my pocket.

I got into the cab of the helicopter while they loaded Rory in the back. I could hear everything that everyone was saying through the headset. It was so surreal. I was terrified, but also incredibly, indescribably calm, still with the two completely separate parts of my brain. And while we flew, I just focused on the horizon and let everything else fall away. "*If he's going to be okay, he's going to be okay. If he's not, he's not.*"

I let the words, *heart beat, lungs move, oxygen flow, brain heal* roll through my mind over and over and over. It was a mantra. The intention I was sending out into the universe. Eyes on the horizon, and complete peace.

I don't know how long the flight took. It felt like forever and yet just an instant. We landed at Levine's Children's hospital and were escorted through a maze into the Pediatric Intensive Care Unit. Rory's care was taken over by the most incredible team of doctors, nurses, and techs. They worked like mad to get him stable, lines placed, machines hooked up, body warming. It was like a brilliant swarm of bees, an intricate dance around his little body, every single soul in the room pouring all of their attention into that tiny human, all of them willing him to live. I sat in the back corner and watched as they buzzed and flitted around the room, trying to save the life of my son.

No one knows, I realized. None of my friends. None of my family. No one knew what was happening but me, and Brock, and his parents.

I took a picture of all of the feet surrounding Rory's hospital bed, and posted online, "*Please send prayers for Rory. Please lift him up. We need your help right now. Please pray for Rory. Send him your love and light and intention.*"

The PICU doctor came over then, and she explained to me what was being done, how things looked, what his prognosis was—not good. She told me her goal was to get him through the next few hours, and to start to warm his body. We wouldn't know what would happen until we got him back up to 98 degrees. We couldn't know anything until then.

Brock arrived minutes later with his brothers. I was shocked—they had come so quickly despite not being in a helicopter. I shared with them everything the doctor had said to me, and since Brock was there to be with Rory, I said I needed to call my mom. I walked out into the hallway and dialed. She answered, and I started crying immediately.

"Mom. Rory fell in the lake. He's unresponsive. He has a heartbeat, but it doesn't look good. We don't know if he's going to make it. Mom..." I didn't know what else to say. The call was breaking up—the signal was poor. I told her I would call her later if there was an update and hung up.

I went back to Brock and we stood next to our baby. He was covered in blankets and a heating apparatus. He had a tube going into his mouth, and tape across his face, but he still looked like our perfect little boy. He was just sleeping so peacefully. We leaned over him and whispered promises to him, reasons to stay. Mama would sleep with him again, and he could nurse all night long. Dada promised that he would take the baby-gate down, and Rory could go into the kitchen whenever he wanted. He could play with all of the big kid toys. *Just stay, Rory. Please choose to stay.* I put my hand on his head and chest, and was again surprised by how cold he was. I asked for a hat and there were none—they didn't have hats of 19 month old size in the PICU. They wrapped a warm pillow case around his head, and I was angry. He looked stupid. Undignified. I wanted a regular hat for him so badly.

Judy and Tim arrived, and sat with us. Everyone was there, crying and hugging and praying. Our kids were at Judy's neighbors house—Nancy was feeding them dinner and watching them. I sat at the end of the bench and felt a crushing emptiness, an unexpected loneliness that shook me to my core. Brock was surrounded by his family, and I was alone. My baby was dying and I was alone. The ache filled my chest and I cried again. I wanted my mom. I wanted my dad. I wanted anyone.

At that very moment, a nurse walked in and asked me if I knew someone named Mira? I was confused. I mean, I did know someone named Mira—she was one of the midwives that ran the Assistant Training—but I had no idea why the nurse was asking me that. It felt very odd and out of place, like she was trying to figure out if she knew me from somewhere. I finally answered, "Yes, I know Mira," and quite suddenly behind her I saw two familiar faces walking towards me. Jillian and Mira—both of the instructors of my midwifery assistant course. They were there, at the hospital. They saw my instagram post and showed up. For me. My heart exploded in my chest, and I was elated.

They wrapped me in hugs, and asked what happened. I cried, and they cried. They touched and held Rory's hands and face. And then they said there was a waiting room full of people hoping to hear news. I didn't fully comprehend that either, but I followed them out into the waiting room, and was utterly shocked when I walked in.

Everyone. I mean, everyone that I knew and loved was there. Jillian and Mira had come in, but Tori was there, and Blair. Rachel and Bella. Michelle. Amber and Laura and Michael. Shayla and Joss. Brock's best friend from high school was there, in the hospital waiting room, waiting for us. Waiting to hear. Waiting for Rory to be okay. I cried and cried and cried, and was surrounded in the biggest hug by so many arms. Everyone gathered around as I explained quickly what had happened, and how Rory looked.

Everyone showed up.

Someone asked if we wanted my mom to fly out, and I said of course. Tickets were arranged and I quickly called her to tell her to be at the airport with her passport in the morning. And then I hugged everyone again but wanted to get back to Rory's side.

The pastor for the church that Brock's family attended came shortly after with food. Chicken noodle soup. We thanked him, and sat. We sat and waited. We sent people home. We told them we would update, and we waited. Every hour, they did blood tests. They were checking his pH levels, and organ functions. They were checking to see if his body was working better or worse. All night, he got better and better. His blood levels kept improving. His body was warming. His heart was beating on its own, and it looked like his organ functions were getting better.

The attending physician came in and did a neurological exam on Rory to test for brain function, and it wasn't good. He had no reactions, no pupil dilation, no blink reflex. She told us gently, honestly, that it didn't look hopeful, but we had hope anyways. His body wasn't warm yet—function could return. We held on to hope for dear life.

She noticed that Rory's feet were jerking, and thought it was possible that he was having seizures, so she ordered an EEG—an electroencephalogram—a brain scan. It didn't take them long to figure out that the jerks were not seizures and so they removed the EEG leads. The next time I went over to him, he smelled like the most awful, toxic glue. I cried. He didn't smell like my boy.

It was after 2am when we were given a room and told to sleep. There was nothing we could do. They would come and get us if anything changed. We checked into the parent sleeping room and I undressed. My sweater and shirt were still damp from the lake. Someone had gone to my house and brought me a change of clothes. I put on pajamas, got into bed and closed my eyes and then... just laid there, wide awake for ages. I couldn't make my brain stop spinning. After about two hours of fitful, useless rest, I finally rolled out of bed and went back to be with Rory. I just wanted to be near him.

I got a coffee, and heard really wonderful news about Rory's labs. Everything was back to nearly the normal range. Laying in the bed together, Brock and I had decided the night before that we were going to continue with hope and believing as long as things continued to improve. Every turn for the better meant that perhaps he was going to stay. But we knew that his body would not heal if he was going to go. The labs—they renewed my hope.

I was asked to leave the room as a tech came in to do a chest x-ray, and then another did a brain CT scan. I knew we would have to wait until around 7am to hear from the doctors about the reports from the x-rays and scans. I asked the nurses for some soap and warm water so I could wash the glue out of Rory's hair.

Almost immediately, two sweet nurses came in with a tub of warm, soapy water and a comb. They cooed and talked sweetly over Rory; told him how beautiful he was; talked about his lashes and his curls. They loved him as they washed the stinky glue out of his hair. I was so grateful, and filled to bursting with love for every person we came into contact with.

At shift change, we got a new crew of nurses and a new doctor, who came in around 7:30. He looked at the CT and X-ray reports, and then he spoke to me frankly. Rory had some very dismal signs. He had developed something called Diabetes Insipidus, which meant that the body was no longer regulating blood sugar, and that his kidneys were just dumping liters and liters of fluid. Rory's x-ray also looked awful. His lungs were bruised and swollen, and they appeared to be filled with fluid—not IN the lungs, but tissue swelling. Edema. Then he looked at me with compassion in his eyes and said, "I'm so sorry, Mrs. Allender. I can't fix his lungs. They just don't have any more to give."

He showed me that the ventilator was on the highest possible settings, with the highest flow of oxygen, and Rory's oxygen saturation numbers were still dropping. His lungs just couldn't move the oxygen into his blood. He told me that maybe there was another, higher-tech ventilator we could try... but it might only give us a few hours. He told me that we could keep fighting and lose him to the machines... or we could unplug the machines and hold him as he went.

Brock came into the room shortly after, and I numbly relayed everything the doctor had said. He was quiet for a few moments, taking it all in, and then we both cried. We knew he was leaving. We knew it was the right thing: to let him go.

We spread the word and updated the people nearest to us. We asked to have our children brought to the hospital—it felt right to let them decide whether or not they were going to say good-bye.

And then we waited. Again. For people to show up and say their farewells. It seemed like forever. I got up in the bed with Rory, and held him, and cried. His body was warm, but sleeping. Lifeless. I held him and watched helplessly as his oxygen saturation levels crept lower and lower. I got angry and frustrated waiting for family to show up, waiting for my children and Judy and Tim to get there. I felt like we were losing him. Waiting to lose him, and losing him. I got unbearably angry when people came into the room to cry at me and over me when I hadn't asked for them. I didn't want them to be there. I was mad when I was asked if they could take his footprints and handprints. *I don't want his footprints. I want him. I want him to be fine. I want him to come home. Don't ask me this. Don't ask this of me.*

Jillian came in and told me that Amber had brought her camera. She told me that I wouldn't be able to answer the question, and that I would never have to look at any pictures if I didn't want to see them, but that she thought I should let Amber take a few. I nodded. I didn't want to need them. I didn't want any of it. But I nodded.

Still we waited. Finally, our kids arrived, and Brock went to tell them that their brother was dying. He didn't know how to do it, or what to say, but he bravely walked towards his children to tell them the hardest thing he could imagine.

And then he brought them in to say goodbye.

Ronan couldn't handle the sadness. He walked into the hospital room and immediately cried out in anxiety and fear. He couldn't stand to be in the room... It was too much for his tender heart.

Ruby walked over slowly, sadly, and put her hand on Rory's belly. I cried out when she told me, "It's okay mama. It's not your fault. It's not anyone's fault." She placed a drawing on the bed beside Rory; a drawing that she had made of our family, with Rory above us as a star. She kissed him and said good-bye.

Four year old Ryder wanted to be on the bed next to me. He was confused and didn't understand. He just wanted his mama, and Rory didn't look like Rory anymore- he was so swollen from all of the fluids and medicines. Ryder wanted to touch Rory; his cheeks, his lips, his eyelids. He pretended to cry, and I told him he didn't have to be sad. He just had to say good-bye to Rory, because Rory wasn't coming home. Ryder said good-bye, and seemed to be completely fulfilled with that. He was carried out of the room.

Judy and Tim arrived shortly after, and I realized that the sun was beginning to go down. It had been nearly 24 hours. I saw that familiar late afternoon glow, and time just seemed to slow down.

The nurses came in and asked if they could "un-wire" my baby. I nodded, and they slowly and lovingly removed all of his lines, IV's, tubes and cords. Lastly, they pulled out the breathing tube and he was free again. Just my baby again. His sweet little body pressed into mine as it had been so many times before, and I could just hold him again. I laid my cheek against his forehead and memorized the way his hair curled off of his skin. The way his eyelashes left his eyes and touched under his brows. The way his hand felt when it touched my face. I pressed his tiny fingers into my cheek over and over. I whispered to him, "I'm sorry... I love you... Please forgive me... Rory, I'm so sorry... I love you..."

Each single moment stretched into hours, and suddenly the room seemed universally huge. Filled with more than just my family, Brock's family. It was filled with light and love. Everything was crystal clear, crystalline and in slow motion. I saw every dust mote and heard every sound. I whispered to him that it was okay for him to go as I felt him fighting to breathe. "You can go, Rory. Please don't stay for me. I will be okay. We will be okay. It's okay to go."

I looked up, around the room at everyone else, their eyes filled with horror and grief and tears. No one looked directly at me, and everyone was hurting. Suddenly, disbelievingly I shouted, "Is this really real?! IS THIS REALLY REAL? IS THIS ACTUALLY FUCKING HAPPENING??"

It felt like the most horrific and awful nightmare that I could imagine, and I couldn't convince myself it was real. My baby. My Rory. My sweet sunshine boy. My little brown baby. His breaths were coming farther and farther apart. They were shorter, and weaker. And then... they were no more. I felt his heart stop beating beneath my hand and I wailed again.

He was gone.

I held him tighter in that moment. I squeezed him harder and held him closer and breathed him in deeper. I didn't want to let him go. I wasn't ready yet. His body was warm and he was my sweet, peaceful, lovely, tiny boy. *I'm sorry. I love you. Please forgive me. I'm sorry. I'm so, so sorry. My Rory. I'm so sorry.*

The doctor came in to listen with a stethoscope, and told us Rory was gone. He sorrowfully announced the time of death, but I knew he was wrong. I knew when my baby left. I felt it.

I held on for another few minutes, and then I had to go. I had to go, and leave the room, and leave the hospital and go. I didn't want to feel his body get cold. I couldn't do it. I left him.

They took me to another room, and brought the kids to see me. I couldn't be with them either, and I asked someone to take the kids somewhere else. Anywhere else. Stay with a friend. Keep them safe. I just couldn't do it.

I was asked if I wanted to see him again and I said no, I didn't. I couldn't. I wanted to go home. My baby was gone, and that body wasn't him, and I didn't need to see it. I just needed to go home.

Mira pulled her car around. I was escorted out of the hospital, supported on both sides as though I was deathly ill, weak and dying. We walked out of the giant glass doors, and I realized that my world had stopped. My baby was gone... Only the sun had not yet set and people were still smiling and I was enraged.

WHY ARE YOU SMILING? HOW CAN THE SUN BE SHINING? DON'T YOU KNOW AN ANGEL HAS JUST DIED? CAN'T YOU SEE THAT MY LIFE HAS BEEN SHATTERED? WHY HASN'T THE WORLD STOPPED WITH US?

I climbed into the car, and Mira took us home. Brock walked in and immediately took down the baby gate. It had been his promise. We sat down on the couch, and looked around our clean, empty house. It had fallen dark. There were no children. There were no signs of life. There was no noise, and no baby mess, and no diapers and no high chairs. We were home, and it felt as though the whole world had ended. I wished it had. I laid my head on Brock's shoulder as he wrapped his arms around me, and together we cried anew.

Our baby died, and we had to keep living.

chapter 13

The minutes and hours and days and weeks after your baby dies are impossible. Not just impossible to survive, but impossible to keep track of, impossible to understand, impossible to line up in a way that makes sense. Surviving the maelstrom of grief becomes a moment to moment exercise. Some of those moments seem to last for hours, to go on without end. But also, there were hours and even days that felt like they flashed by in an instant. Because of this, the timeline of healing gets… fuzzy. Warped. It seems to bulge out in some places, and narrow down to a thread in others. Please bear with me as you read through these next chapters and find yourself disoriented with the way time appears to be passing—it's not a mistake, nor because I couldn't figure out a better way to do it. It is simply and most honestly because this is the nature of grief, time is made up, and you just sort of have to hang on for the ride.

At some point, while we were in the hospital with Rory, well meaning friends made their way into our house to clean it for us. It was well known by that point that we were under a Department of Social Services investigation (as I believe all accidental deaths are) and there would be an upcoming DSS visit. Everything was made ready; the kitchen was cleaned, the floors tidied, the beds made. Sheets were washed, and then windows. All of the laundry was done. In a moment of loving care, these well meaning friends thought that seeing Rory's high-chair and car-seat and toys and diapers would be painful, so they were all removed.

When I walked into my house from the hospital after holding my baby as he died, my shattered heart was astounded all over again. The breath left my body and I couldn't put two thoughts together—I glanced around and all traces of Rory had been erased. No smudgy handprints on the windows. The sweaty baby smell was gone from his bed. His seat at the table and his place in our car were all gone. His place in our home, in our life, had been wiped away. I didn't even have any pictures of him hanging on the wall (fourth child problems) and I couldn't shake the feeling. It was as though he had never existed.

He was gone. Poof. Just like that, gone. His heart stopped beating, and the hospital kept his dead body, and my mind and soul couldn't comprehend it. Gone. Like a candle snuffed out, and all that was left of it was the imprint of the flame in a retina.

Gone.

I longed to hold him, ached to grasp something he left behind; to cuddle a pillow or a blanket or a bear that smelled of his smell. His laundry was gone. All of his clothes, clean and dirty, were missing from my house. I wished it had never been done. I raged that it was. Time would have done that soon enough. It would have been so much safer to leave everything as it lay, exactly as it was before he left.

He was not there and there was nothing of his for us to hold onto, so we crawled into bed and held on to each other.

"This is no one's fault," I said quietly into Brock's shoulder.

"What do you mean?" He pulled his head back to look at me.

I shrugged, "I mean... I don't think we can blame someone for this happening. You know? It wasn't anyone's fault. It just... happened."

Brock nodded. I was immediately relieved to know that he had been thinking and feeling the same things.

"I don't blame you, babe," I told him as tears filled my eyes. He hugged me tightly to him, and whispered into my neck, "I don't blame you either."

Before long, we both passed out from grief and exhaustion,

wrapped in each other's arms and in a desperately empty bed that used to hold a sweaty little boy and now felt just so empty.

My eyes opened the next morning, and immediately the world crashed down around me.

Oh my god, my baby died.

My whole body was sore, stiff and achy and refused to move right, although whether from exertion, time in the hospital, or simply grief, I could not know.

I didn't want to get out of bed. I was alone, and I didn't want to get up into a world where my Rory was no longer alive and I had to keep living without him. I felt no drive, no physical urge; not hunger, nor thirst, nor desire to go pee. Everything was numb.

Doing absolutely nothing didn't feel like an option, though. I didn't know where Brock was, or if he had slept. Eventually, I dressed and made my way downstairs. I was aware the day before that my mother had been contacted, and someone had bought her a plane ticket. I knew that she was coming—I had been told—but the shock, surprise and comfort I felt upon walking into my kitchen to see her there took my breath away. She wrapped her arms around me and I sobbed and sobbed into her warmth. It was surreal that my mother was there with me, but Rory was not.

Brock was sipping coffee at the dining room table where he was talking with Jillian. She had shown up for us again, the assistant midwife at our home births, turned teacher, turned support. We needed to make funeral home arrangements, and decide what we were doing with the body, and she had come to help.

The body. Rory's body. My baby's body.

There was an obituary to write, and people to notify, and the press were swarming like wasps—angry and violent and clamoring to break the story of what happened to the little boy in the lake. They wanted us to release a statement or maybe do an interview.

Please don't ask this of me. I cannot. Please.

My mother put food in front of me, and I ate eggs and toast although I felt no hunger and there was no taste. The numbness was completely oppressive, overwhelming. My phone was blowing up with text messages and alerts; the news of Rory's death had broken on Instagram and my followership was increasing by the thousands. I didn't have the bandwidth or the energy to deal with any of it, so I just left it face down on the table.

I looked around my home, and was again devastated to find no evidence that Rory had ever even lived; no proof that he was real, no marks that he'd made. It was as though he had been erased completely.

There was a knock on the door. I didn't move to go get it. I didn't do anything. I just sort of existed and people came to me. My mom answered the knock, and I heard her say, "No, we aren't interested." And then more firmly, "We are NOT interested."

Brock got up and walked over and just closed the door. It didn't take long to figure out who it was—it was the press. Again. Reporters and camera people that were bound and determined to get our statement. It felt cheap, and false, and gross.

Those words—the 'statement'—that wasn't what they really wanted. What they wanted was the grief. The horror. The agony. They wanted tears and turmoil. They wanted to broadcast our pain for everyone to see—and not because it was good or necessary, but because it got lots and lots of views. The way that the news crews pushed for the story and canvassed both the neighborhood where we lived, and the neighborhood at the lake for anyone to tell them what had happened... It made me sick to my stomach.

We agreed that we weren't going to talk to any press. We weren't willing to sacrifice ourselves and our hearts on the altar of greater North American morbid curiosity. Instead, we had a conversation about what it could look like to 'break the story' our own way. The whole picture. A human way. I didn't know what to do yet, but I was sure it would come to me.

Brock's mom and dad came by the house that first evening to check on us, and we sat down at the table together. Because of the conversation we'd had in bed the night before, Brock and I made it clear to his parents that we both fully agreed, that no one was *at fault* for Rory's death. There could be no guilt and no blame. We didn't want them, or Brady, or either of us being accused—blame wouldn't bring him back and would only tear everyone apart. Nothing would bring him back. We wholeheartedly absolved each other of all culpability, and extended that gift to everyone present that day.

Then we also agreed that the water wasn't at fault. It wasn't the lake, and it wasn't the house, and it wasn't the fact that we were there that day. There were multiple ways to look at the reason for Rory leaving, and the ones that were most comfortable, and easiest to digest, were the ones where it was always what was meant to happen. Part of his purpose. Ordained since the beginning of time. Not something we could command or control or subvert just because we wanted him to stay. If love were enough, if wanting and pleading and praying and begging were enough, he would have stayed.

Our third and last agreement and choice at the table that evening was that, no matter what, Brock and I weren't going to let the death of our son destroy our marriage. We had already come through so much, and worked so hard on being together and being in love; we weren't going to let our children lose their little brother and then also lose their family. We agreed that we would be together in grief, always. If one of us was crying or sad, the other would come and meet there. If we were lonely or hurting or aching, we would say it out loud. No emotions were off limits, and no time was bad for whatever was coming up. No one else lost our baby but us.

Maybe those things don't feel like choices, but I truly believe that they are. Sometimes our feelings—the hard, powerful, dark ones try to convince us that we don't have a choice; "I could never go there again," or, "I could never forgive them," or, "There is no way I could ever let my kids swim again." Those feelings seem immutable, but truly they *are* choices. Brock and I knew that we wanted to choose to do things differently.

At the table that day, we told Judy and Tim that we didn't want them to feel responsible for what happened just because they lived on the lake, and we definitely didn't want them to sell the house. Judy immediately burst into tears, and confessed that she had been so scared that we would feel the opposite. She had been terrified that we would blame her, blame them, blame everything.

Despite the fact that we had been on the verge of removing Brock's parents from our daily lives, it suddenly seemed like we were all on the same page and far more connected than we had ever been before.

Finally, it was bedtime again. We had survived the first whole day without our son, and it was time to try to sleep again. Time to lay in bed and miss and hurt and grieve and flashback to the day of Rory's death again. I dreaded going to bed. I was given a prescription of Ativan to help with sleep, but I knew that I didn't want to need it. I knew that I wanted to be able to sleep on my own at some point, so I figured that I just wouldn't take them. Instead, I just laid there for hours and hours, until I finally succumbed to the exhaustion.

chapter 14

I woke up the second morning, and there was a tiny moment, just an instant where I forgot. Why does my body ache? Why are my eyes so sore? Why is my throat scratchy?

Oh my god, my baby died.

And there it was. I woke up to reality. My baby died, and I cried again.

But throughout that second day, the pangs of grief started coming farther and farther apart. I was thankful for the reprieve, but simultaneously I was already resisting the idea that the pain of his loss could fade.

How could this ever stop hurting??

As I started to notice the amount of time that grew between the deep, painful, pressures of the waves of grief, I reflected on the idea that it felt somewhat like contractions.

Contractions.

Because Rory died relatively soon after he was born—not so soon that I was still feeling the dregs of his birthing, but not so long that I had forgotten it altogether—the idea of the parallels and reflections between birth and death were just so plainly evident to me. I sat there in bed and pondered.

The moment that Rory died was utter agony. Pressure and pain and intensity and so much transformative power that I couldn't be with it. I thought it was going to kill me.

Gosh, just like the moment of his birth.

The moments after his death, the pain returned—over and

over again. A shuddering, crushing pain that reminded me that he was gone. They were so close I could hardly catch my breath. They squeezed the air out of my lungs. I could not keep up.

Gosh, just like the final moments of labor. Just like transition.

As I thought about it, my painful contractions spacing farther and farther apart, I imagined as though his dying was a mirror image of his birthing, the moment of birth and the moment of death being the apex of each other, and rippling outwards away from the peak.

Holy shit, I thought, *his coming and his going felt exactly the same.*

The pain. The terror. The deep black hole. It was all there, present in his dying and his birthing.

As I wandered down the path of the mirror image that death seems to be for birth, I started to awaken to another epiphany: the same mirror image reflection of knowing your person before their birth, and after their death.

What I had come to know was this, with certainty: that when your unborn child is inside of you—you do not know them. They are there, and you can feel them, but you can't see them and don't know them yet. You long to know them, and wonder and wish and while away your time imagining what they will be like, but you *can't know them.*

However, the absolute instant they are born, as soon as they cross the portal into this world, they are immediately *known to you,* and you can *never un-know them.*

It's staggering. It's as though they have always existed and will always exist, and now they are here and you see them and feel them and smell them and you KNOW them. You forever know them.

Death, somehow, is the mirror image of that. The inverse of it. You have had your person. You love them deeply, and already you *forever know them.* No world exists where you do not know them. Except, now that they are gone, you can no longer see them. You can no longer hold or feel or touch them, and your knowing fills you with the desperate need to wrap your arms around something that isn't there anymore. You wonder and wish and while away that time trying to imagine what it would be like if they were still here—because you KNOW them and you can't see them anymore. No smell, no touch, no sound—all that's left is the knowing, and it can never be un-known.

The echoes and the parallels and the mirroring is not a mistake, I think. And I feel like Rory's birth and death were exactly far enough apart for me to be able to see those ripples. It's hard for me to believe that was an accident. I think I was meant to know it—that birth and death are the same—just mirror images of each other.

I just kept waiting for things to go dark. I had spent so much of the last ten years seeking the light, and I was sure that losing Rory was going to absolutely blot out the sun. If anything was powerful enough to usher in a return to depression, it would certainly be child loss.

Only, it didn't happen. Even when I was ready for it. Even while I was expecting it. It didn't go dark. I stayed in the light, and walked around somewhat wild-eyed. Surprised. I guess what all the books and healers and teachers had said was true—that my journey was mine, healing was progress, and there was no going backwards.

The fog of grief, however, was thick, and obscured almost everything. It affected the way that I thought, and the way that I talked. I was unable to make decisions, or care for myself, or hold up my end of conversations. It was as though all of the walls and barriers that I had spent my life erecting to make myself feel safe and acceptable in life had been stripped away, and I was just purely me; unveiled and unguarded and completely okay with it.

I unapologetically said whatever popped into my mind, whether it was polite or not. "No, I'm not doing that." "That looks stupid." "I want it to be this way." "This food is absolutely disgusting." I wasn't intentionally trying to be rude. I had just been such an ingrained people-pleaser my whole life, I didn't have the energy to do it anymore. I couldn't make anyone else happy. I couldn't even soften the blows.

One of the most unfortunate truths of child loss is that the mother is typically deeply surrounded in love and support and community; and dads are not.

Brock felt mostly invisible in the days after Rory's death. His phone wasn't blowing up with text messages and his social media wasn't awash with worry and concern. The guests that showed up at our house were rarely for him, and while he received a whole host of hugs, almost never was he the focus of compassion nor attention.

That second afternoon, there was an unexpected knock at the door. Truly, by this point, unexpected knocks were almost expected—we had had so many unannounced visitors and solicitors that it was almost laughable. Anyhow, there was a knock at the door, and again I did not answer. I heard hugs and sniffles coming from the front of the house, and waited to see who would appear as they were welcomed into our home.

My breath was almost completely taken away as Brock's two best friends, Mitch and Jake, walked in with their wives. Best friends may be a bit of a misnomer. Brock's Former Best Friends? Brock's Biggest Heartache?

At one time, the six of us had been a gang. Brock, Mitch and Jake all grew up together and were like the three Musketeers. They bummed around together, played sports together, partied together. Their friendships had survived attending different colleges, a decade of distance, even a multitude of girlfriends. As couples, we had weekly, or at least monthly date nights, lake days, dinner get-togethers, and even camping trips.

Brock and I were the first in the group to get married (Mitch and Jake were Brock's groomsmen, Angela and Donna were my bridesmaids.). We were also the first to have children. When Ronan came, Mitch and Jake were uncles, and it was sweet. When Ruby came, just a handful of days before Ronan's second birthday, the ladies showed up and planned a birthday party for our son, because we couldn't.

And then… they stopped showing up.

They stopped calling and inviting us to events. They stopped hanging out with Brock. We found out, after the fact, that we had been excluded from group hangouts and date nights that continued to happen without us.

I was heartbroken. For myself, but mostly for Brock. In a desperate attempt to mend things that I assumed were my fault, I wrote a long and tender email asking for clarity and forgiveness. That it was obvious that we had done something wrong, and would do anything to fix it. I just wanted to understand and be given the chance to mend whatever it was that caused the rift. I poured my heart out in that letter, and it was met with resounding silence.

They ghosted us.

So when they showed up at our home just after our fourth child died, I was not delighted to see them.

I was fucking enraged.

They walked in looking somber and contrite, and I couldn't keep the rage out of my voice nor off of my face. I stood up in challenge, not in welcome. "Why are you here?" I demanded.

Four sets of eyes widened in shock, and they looked back and forth at each other in discomfort.

"We are so sorry…"

"Rory…"

"We can't imagine…"

Mumbles and murmurs of words that were meant to bring comfort or explanation that just made me angrier.

You didn't know Rory.

You didn't care that he was born.

You weren't a part of his life.

You do not belong here.

I was seething. Boiling with rage. Some part of me was happy that Brock had someone show up for him, that there was some love and support directly pointed towards him, but all I could access in that moment was anger.

I blinked a few times, shook my head in disbelief, and stated, "I'm really sorry that our baby had to die in order for you to care."

I turned on my heel, and walked away.

They weren't there for me, anyways.

chapter 15

My eyes opened. The third day.
A moment.
Oh my god, my baby died.

On the third day, my children came home. They had been sleeping at various friends' homes. I was not aware where they were, and I could not make myself care. I knew they were safe and loved, and I had had no space for them at all.

But then they were home, and the abyss of grief had to let up. I was still a mother. I had to mother my children. I was immediately angry and resentful. I didn't want to have to meet their needs, or talk them through their emotions, or explain how I was feeling. I didn't want to have to hide my grief to make them comfortable. Shadows of my former resistance to the realities of parenthood started rearing their ugly heads.

I struggled with my emotions as I adjusted to having them in the house… But the truth made itself known. I loved my children deeply, and gratitude that they were alive and present and with me asserted itself over the shades of frustration. My kids wanted to be home, and I wanted them to be home, and they were ALIVE, and I would never again take that for granted.

Despite my always wide open, intensely sensitive nature, in addition to the depth of grief, we decided unwisely to go to Target. I'm not even entirely sure what for—something to do, or something to get. There was some unassailable reason that we needed to go, and I made the decision to go along. I didn't really have any reason to believe that it was a bad idea. It didn't take me long to figure out that that assumption was wrong.

Mom and Brock and the kids and I walked through the store. The lights were so bright and sharp and aggressive—not any different than normal, I was just experiencing them differently. All of the stimuli, both real and energetic, pierced straight into me. The sounds of the multitudes of people, mindlessly living their lives, not caring about children that died, and not immediately aware of the stark mortality that surrounded all of us. It was deafening.

The smells of the bakery and the coffee shop assaulted my overwrought senses. Everywhere I looked, I was shocked by the reality of life on the planet. So many humans. So intensely being. So much potential for pain. I had the unbearable burden of knowing that not a single one of the Target people, moving and living and breathing still, had any idea that my baby had lived or died and was now gone from the world.

I immediately knew that I couldn't be there long, and pushed myself to continue, leaning on Brock as I found myself weaker and weaker with grief. I tilted my head back and whispered up to him with tears in my eyes, "This was a bad idea. I'm not ready." He nodded, understanding deeply and feeling similar things himself.

I was so disconnected from the reality of the moment that I didn't know if we had even found any of the things we came for, but with his agreement, we turned towards the exit. I glanced to my right, and right next to us was a young mother pushing a cart with a baby in the seat; a dreamy little brown boy, with a fluff of hair and dark, dark eyes. He wasn't Rory—in fact, the resemblance didn't reach beyond the skin and eye color—but it was enough to send a spasm of pain through me, to set my heart to pounding and my eyes to watering. A sob escaped my lips, and I quickly turned away from them, burying my face in Brock's chest and simply breaking.

The sweet boy and his mother were never even aware that we were there, nor the reaction that their appearance had evoked. Brock held me as I shattered in the middle of the aisle at Target, quietly sobbing into his chest. He held me until the greater part of the storm passed, and squeezed me gently. I couldn't meet his eyes; I was sad and ashamed of my inability to be in the world. "Let's go," he whispered into my hair. I nodded, and we moved on.

For no explainable reason, and without rational thought, I suddenly reached out and grabbed a 1000 piece jigsaw puzzle of a giant castle on the edge of a cliff, hovered over by a big, dangerous looking dragon off the shelf that we were standing next to and threw it into the cart. I had no idea why, it wasn't even lovely or comforting—just some intuitive urge—and purchased what would become our grief puzzle.

When we got home, and settled back into our safe cocoon, I was able to get a handle on the shame and pain of public grief. I poured how it felt out to Brock, and he assured me it made sense. We didn't have to go back out again. Well, not soon at least.

With not much else to do, we dumped out the puzzle onto the table, and I allowed myself to be with my family, and the friends that showed up to be with us. It was then, in those quiet, peaceful family moments that I experienced an entirely different kind of grief—the first time I smiled again. The first time I laughed. *How can I feel joy when my baby is gone??* It felt like betrayal. It felt like I wasn't honoring how horrific it was that my son had died. On the heels of the first bout of laughter, I felt a heavy rock of shame in my gut. I wanted to punish myself for being happy. Like I needed to cry 15 times to make up for every smile.

The thing is, rationally, I knew I didn't want to *stay* in the sorrow. I didn't want to hurt forever. And I didn't think Rory would want us to hurt forever. Despite all of the aching, we wanted to move towards healing, towards happiness again. It seemed like it was impossible, but that felt like a choice, too.

That evening, after those momentary flashes of joy, Brock and I were laying in bed, wrapped in each other's arms, sharing all of the grief and all of the hard places we had been that day. We intended to make it a habit to connect every evening; to unload the heavy things, and to be with each other—to make sure neither of us felt alone.

We talked about the shame and betrayal of finding joy again—we were both feeling it. And we talked about wanting to go through our grief with our whole hearts, not limiting ourselves to only feeling the bad, hard things. We wanted to allow and accept and invite the brightness and the laughter and the gratitude and the love into our lives again. And we agreed, quietly and tenderly, that we also wanted to move forward loving each other deeply and truly and physically. At that moment, it felt so *wrong* to make love—such a life affirming act—we acknowledged that it was possibly the best thing we could do—to root ourselves in life, and in each other.

And so, we did.

Another whole day of our lives without Rory, and yet still just the third day, and it was finally time to try to sleep again. Brock has never a day in his life had trouble sleeping, but I was struggling nightly. I had been given a bottle of Ativan to help with that impossible task, and I took a half a pill the first night home from the hospital.

The second night, I made the decision to abstain from the sleeping meds. I knew that I was going to want to be able to fall asleep on my own for the rest of my life, and I made the choice against medication so I could start working on it right away.

That night, the third night, as I was lying still and trying to convince my brain to fall into peaceful slumber without drugs, I started hearing words in my head—lines of what felt like a poem. It was as though my brain were coming up with, of its own accord, the most beautiful way to tell the world that my son had died. I laid there with my eyes closed and thought my way through the poem, word for word. When I reached the end, it started over again at the beginning. The same words, the same lines. I immediately pulled out my phone and began typing it out. It felt important.

The following morning, the fourth day, I woke up and shared the poem with everyone that showed up at my home that day; I shared it with them and told them that I wanted to post it on my social media and blog, with a picture of Rory's last moments. It made perfect sense to me. I was going to break the story my way, what had happened to our son, and how it actually was. How it felt to walk through it. Not just the terror and the horror. Not just the rubbernecking. It wasn't going to be like a car wreck on the 9 o'clock news. It was going to be beautiful.

From the first moment I suggested it, everyone begged me not to. They said it was a terrible idea, and that people would be cruel. They said it was unwise to put myself out there in that way. They said that nothing good would come from being that honest. And for a whole moment, I paused and wondered if they were right. But in the end, the pull inside me to share it was stronger than I could account for, and I knew I wasn't wrong. It was just so sure. So I published the poem-story on Instagram and Facebook, and hoped that people would be kind.

Five adults
Four children.
A beautiful day.
Everyone helping. Talking. Loving.
Kids playing in the drive with old toys.
New treasures.
Back turned for a moment: lend a hand.
Out of sight.
Cannot see him.
Cannot hear him.
Run through the open door:
"Is he with you? Do you have him?"
Just a moment, not more.
"He's not inside!" I yell, and everyone moves.
Down to the lake.
Just in case.
Just in case.
I thump around the path and down to the water on stiff legs, tightened with fear.
Scan the glassy surface, smooth as the eye can see, but for a break.
Just a break.
Surely not.
I step up onto the boardwalk.
I see him.
Still.
I scream. And scream. And scream.
As I run to him and pull him from the water, I scream.
Brock tears to us, fast as a blink, to hold him with me.
Yelling, "CALL 911!" his voice icy with terror.
Squeeze his chest, tip him, clear the water.
He is cold, but he is not blue.
No pulse. Tilt head. Breath. Breath.
One two three four five six seven eight nine ten eleven twelve thirteen fourteen fifteen.
Breath. Breath.
I clear vomit from his mouth over and over.
I breathe into his tiny mouth for him, and pump his heart.
I move his oxygen. He is not blue.
Breath. Breath.
Compressions and breaths and clearing his airway.
I hear his lungs fill. I move his blood.
Someone comes to help.
Then EMS arrives.
I fall away from my baby as I let them take over. Hundreds of rounds of CPR and now I just watch.
My steel resolve disappears and I am keening and wailing. Screaming and sobbing.
My baby. My baby.
Brock holds me. My sobs join with his. We can't look at each other.
Only at our baby.
They work and work. They fight for him.
We ride to the hospital in an ambulance. We beg him to come back.
Please choose to stay, Rory kai.
Minutes in the ER. Minutes like hours.
The doctor comes out.
"I've got a heartbeat."
We scream our relief and joy and disbelief. He is not gone.
He is not gone.

Airlifted to the children's hospital by a team of airmen fueled by love and kindness.
The most amazing team of doctors and nurses and therapists.
They keep him alive.
They stabilize him.
I can touch him. Hold him. Kiss him.
Brock puts his hand on Rory's head and whispers sweet words.
Promises.
You can go in the kitchen whenever you want, buddy.
We warm his body. He was hypothermic. His brain function may return as he warms.
It may not.
We didn't know it then, but we were gifted 24 hours with our sweet boy.
Enough time to hold him and kiss him and fill him full of all of our sweet love.
His brothers and sister come to see him.
They cry. But they smile. They love him.
They will miss him.
He is slowly fading.
His lungs can give no more.
We nod when asked, and they pull out his tubes.
He is just my baby now.
Lying in my arms.
He breathes. Again and again, he fights.
He gasps.
I ache.
Brock sobs.
It hurts to watch him.
It's okay to go, Rory.
You can stop fighting.
Thank you.
I love you.
I'm sorry.
Please forgive me.
Please forgive me.
You can go. I will be okay.
My hand on his chest as he slips away.
My lips on his face over and over.
I need to remember how he feels.
I need to never forget.
I hold his hand to my cheek one last time. His sweet fingers on my skin.
In a single instant, his body is no longer alive and yet I am sure—
I am SURE
He is not gone.
He is not gone.
He is only different.
We love you Rory Kai.
Thank you for allowing us to be your parents.
We love you now, then, and always.
I'm sorry we could not save you.
Please forgive us.
Please forgive us.
Please forgive us.

—MANDY ALLENDER, 2017

I pressed publish and then put down my phone and walked away. I didn't want to know how it was received. I was sure it was the right thing, and yet I was terribly afraid that it wasn't. I knew that I couldn't control what the spirits of social media and the internet would do with it, but I needed it to exist outside of my body. It was possible that the world would be kind... it was possible that they would ravage me.

Because that is another hard fucking truth. When you are a parent whose child has died in an accidental manner—you do not feel worthy of anything. You do not feel worthy of love and kindness. It feels absolutely massively wrong for people to want to care for you, and care about you, and let you know that they truly do care.

Despite our agreements and choices to absolve each other of blame, we deeply, truly felt like we should be punished. That shame and derision more neatly fit the bill. That no one, absolutely no one, should be attempting to make things better or ease our suffering in any way because — we had one job. That's how it felt. We had one single, unshakeable job as parents, and that was to keep our children safe. For them to come out alive. That's it. The bar on the floor, basement expectation, single prime directive, and we failed to do even that. We failed to keep him safe, and we failed to bring him back, and we failed him unto his death, and so, we deserved to suffer.

But it's not true.

Let me say that again. **It's not true.** None of it. Not any of it. It's not true that we deserved shame and derision. It's not true that we should've been punished instead. It is not true that we merited nothing but pain and suffering, that no one should be allowed to help. None of those feelings hold even a modicum of truth.

It took us a while to get there. Accepting kindness and love in the face of our failure was one of the hardest things we've ever had to do. It would have been easier to accept cruelty and abuse. But instead, we opened our eyes and our hearts and our arms to the possibility that what happened wasn't our fault, and that truly kind people just wanted to help in any way they could.

I picked up my phone later that night, after sharing the poem. I held my breath and guarded my heart. I was so ready for the anger and derision I had been warned against.

I gasped softly instead.

They weren't cruel, they were kind.

They weren't cruel, they were lovely.

They weren't cruel, they were wonderful.

Absolutely wonderful.

I did not expect, not even a little bit, the tsunami of love and support, passion and compassion, understanding and empathy that were poured over us. Hundreds of comments, thousands of messages. Sorrow and empathy. Tears upon tears upon tears; all for Rory, all for us. The massive, unbelievable tidal wave of everything good and positive and beautiful that could be offered to parents who just lost their child to an accidental death. To folks who didn't believe they were worthy. To people just barely keeping their heads and hearts above it all.

The list of the kindness and love and compassion that we were shown was long, and wide, and deep. Gifts, stories, words, pictures, paintings, meals, plants, letters—someone had a star named for Rory Kai and it is forever in the star registry in the Pegasus galaxy. Someone adopted an endangered Sea Turtle in his name. Yet another someone else had a brick dedicated for him in the Children's Walk in Charlotte. If you will believe it, I was gifted a whole entire tattoo—someone had purchased a credit at a tattoo studio and gifted it to me so I could create a memorial tattoo if I should want to.

We realized that, in allowing others to help us, we were also allowing them to feel *able to help*. We gave them the gift of doing something meaningful. None of it actually made anything better, and yet all of it helped. It's so hard to explain, so hard to understand, the paradox of help. But believe me, it is both.

Above all, the greatest gift I received from publishing the poem online was that nearly every person I knew or met from that point forward had already read what had happened to Rory, and it saved me from having to re-explain, and re-share, and retell the story over and over and over. And that was the kindest possible thing I ever could have done for myself.

chapter 16

Five days.

Five days after Rory died, Ruby turned six years old.

Six isn't a particularly special birthday. It's not really a milestone of any kind, like turning five (one whole hand!) or ten (double digits!). It's not the entrance to the teen years, or the farewell to childhood. It really isn't that remarkable at all—except that it was Ruby's first time turning six. And it was the oldest she'd ever been before. And her baby brother had just died.

Leading up to Ruby's sixth birthday, Brock and I had a conversation. Probably many conversations, or a continuing narrative, but what we discussed was somehow singular and manifold at the same time—that our children had lost their brother, but they were not also going to lose their parents, their family, their home. We also reminded ourselves that our remaining children *were still alive.* And in that, we could do nothing less than celebrate them, cherish them, and revel in their aliveness.

That does NOT mean it was easy. There was definitely a part of my soul that continued to be exceedingly angry that I had to put aside my grief for a day, and pretend that I wasn't hollow to the depths of my being, that I wasn't gutted and wracked and wrecked. I was resentful that I had to smile. It had only been five days. But that was just the smallest part of me. I hushed that part. What I allowed to come forth was joy and gratitude—Ruby deserved that. She deserved the day to be whole, and hers alone.

When my kids were small, I didn't want the focus on birthdays to be the presents—I wanted it to be the person. I wanted each child to feel like THEY were being celebrated that day, and the day was theirs. From the moment they rose in the morning, until they were tucked lovingly into bed, their birthdays were meant to be a celebration of the fact that they existed. Our tradition included whatever they wanted for breakfast, so my mama whipped up pancakes with sprinkles. Then Ruby asked Gramma to use my guitar so we could all sing together—Ruby knew that Gramma had the most beautiful voice. We sat in the living room and sang until mom's fingers were blistered and it was time for lunch.

My mother, and my dear friend Rachel and I took Ruby out for lunch at her favorite restaurant with her best friend Grace. She got the biggest milkshake I'd ever seen. The smile on her face and the sparkle in her eyes were a breath of fresh air. It was plain to see that the sadness had been wearing on her, and that day—her birthday—she was thriving in just being a kid again. She laughed and clapped in joy as the wait-staff came out and sang her happy birthday. She skipped joyfully, hand in hand with Grace, out of the restaurant and back to the car. "Next, I want to go see a movie!"

I could tell that I was running out of bandwidth—it was still really hard to be out in public while internally I just wanted to be at home, crying in bed. But. It was her birthday. So we drove to the movie theater, and looked at the listings. The only kid appropriate movie that was playing on that particular February 10th was, "Sing"—a friendly little animation about a group of animals putting on a theater performance in order to save their beloved stage from demolition. It was supposed to be incredibly sweet, and have great music.

Because of the newness of my loss, and the relatively short amount of time that had passed since Rory drowned, I had not yet had the experience of being publically triggered. I never would have expected "Sing" to have a near-drowning scene, nor would I have been able to guess how terribly that experience would shake me; sitting in the theater, calm and pleasant, enjoying the film… and then suddenly having a panic attack, unable to breathe for the constriction in my chest and the sobs that were clogging themselves in my throat.

It had never occurred to me how traumatic it could be to have the mode of my child's death be displayed for public consumption. Suddenly, I realized how often that must occur for bereaved parents, and all bereaved persons alike. How often did a depicted car crash horrify family members of car-crash victims? How often did kidnapping or heart attack or tragic accident send someone into a spiral of pain and jagged memory? In that painful moment, I hated the media—all media. I hated that people wanted to consume tragedy for entertainment. I hated how blithely and benignly our culture happily took in what was quite literally a depiction of the worst moments and worst memories of someone's life—just to be entertained.

I should have gotten up and left, but I didn't want Ruby to know that I was upset. I didn't want to ruin her special day. Instead, I just shut my eyes and clenched my fists, and tried to slow my breathing down. *It's okay. You know that he dies.* Rachel reached out to hold my hand, and we waited for the moment to pass. It did. The girls were blissfully unaware, and entirely unaffected by the moment that nearly took me out at the knees.

We finished the movie with no other issues and took Ruby for the last part of her special celebration day: across the street to Target where she was allowed to pick out any gift that she wanted.

I had already failed at this particular Target, and the store itself was its own special kind of torture. For the last handful of years, every time I took the kids to Target, I would have them sit on the curb in front of what I called 'the photo wall.' I shared all of the pictures on Instagram, and eventually created a hashtag that we lovingly dubbed #thetargetwallseries.

Clicking on that hashtag would bring up images of all four of my children from minuscule and chubby and cute, getting bigger and taller and slimmer. Losing teeth and getting leggy. Sweet tiny newborn Rory held safely in his biggest brother's arms. Ryder pouting because he wanted to hold the baby. Ruby smiling because she got to hold Rory's hand. Picture after picture after picture of my bright, beautiful, brilliant kiddos growing up… and there would never be another picture of all four of my children. I apologized to Ruby and told her I just had to wait in the car.

When we got home and got the kids settled into bed, I broke again. Being out in public was hard. Being around people, and their wide open energy was hard. Seeing people (animated or not) struggling to breathe under water was unbelievably hard. Celebrating Ruby was essential and necessary and it was all just so damn hard.

chapter 17

Mom was there with us when DSS arrived. Because Rory's death was accidental, there was an automatic Department of Social Services case opened, and we had to undergo an official investigation.

The lady from the DSS office was a young black woman, sweet and incredibly soft spoken. When I opened the door to let her in, I was struck by her beauty; so profound, and yet made gentle by her nature. I expected to be grilled, to be shamed, to be put through the ringer. Instead, when Miss Lana walked in, she immediately apologized for our loss. My eyes filled with tears at the unexpected kindness. Her eyes filled with compassion as she told us that it felt awful that she had to do this type of investigation. "I can clearly see that y'all are good people, good parents." The energy with which she entered my home and spoke to us was an immediate balm on my big, scary fears.

Miss Lana assured us that she would just have to ask all of the questions required, and we'd get together several times over the next few weeks, and as long as everything went as predicted, the case would be closed and there was nothing to worry about.

Brock and I were subdued, reserved. It was surreal to have her in our home. It was painful. Even though she reminded us over and over that no one wanted to take our other children away, just her presence was a different kind of reminder. That our baby died, and even though innocent until proven guilty is a lovely theory, that's not how it actually works—or feels.

Brock squeezed my hand as we sat down at the table across from Miss Lana, the light falling severely across her gentle face, giving it a hardness that belied her peaceful nature. I took a deep breath, and Brock and I settled into answering her litany of required questions. They were all pretty simple, "Have you ever..." and "Do you ever..." and "Would you ever..." in relation to drugs, abuse, and neglect. Each question came with a jolt of fear—it's not that they were implicitly dangerous or difficult questions; just that they carried with them the idea that 'this could be the one where we say the thing that makes her take our children away.'

The thing was, we knew we weren't perfect parents. There were lots of moments in our parenting history that we weren't proud of, or wish we had done differently. But also? Also, we had a home filled with smart, bright, beautiful, loving children that we would do anything for. We loved them to distraction. They had clean clothes, and nourishing food. We spent time and energy talking to them, teaching them, getting to know them. We apologized when we were wrong. We weren't perfect parents... but we were good parents. We were just also hoping that we were *good enough*.

"I think that's all of the questions I have for you," Ms. Lana said as she smiled shyly into her paperwork. Eye contact seemed to be uncomfortable for her, and she preferred to look at her documents. "Is there someone else I could ask a few questions of?" My mother immediately volunteered, and I was surprised that she was willing to allow Brock and I to stay in the room as the secondary interview happened.

Ms. Lana then proceeded with a similar line of questioning, asking my mom if she'd ever seen us punish or discipline our kids beyond a reasonable amount, or leave bruises or marks on our children's bodies. (She had not.) She asked if mom had ever seen us doing drugs. (She had not!) She asked about the food we fed the kids, and whether or not they seemed excessively hungry. (They were not.) Mom vehemently agreed or denied as was appropriate. A part of me was amused, as my mom and dad had only spent a handful of days with my children over the eight years we'd been parents, but it was fine. She knew we were good.

Ms Lana then asked if, to my mother's knowledge, Brock or I had ever left the kids home alone for more than four hours at a time without checking on them.

Brock and I looked at each other in shock, our eyes completely wide with disbelief. At that moment, I jumped in and asked, "Wait a minute. Are you telling me that, up until this point in our lives, we would have been within our rights as parents to leave our kids home completely alone as long as it was for under four hours of time?" Ms Lana nodded in the affirmative, and I shook my head slowly back and forth, unable to digest that information.

"Completely alone? Like, alone in the house all by themselves? The ages they are right now?" She nodded again.

I spread my hands out on the table, arms pressed down as though they were holding up my disbelief, "Are you telling me that I could run to the grocery store and get groceries for my family while I leave my children at home unaccompanied… and I have been dragging FOUR CHILDREN to the grocery store instead? Every single time??"

I gasped as I said it, and realized that I would never again have four children to take anywhere, but the sentiment wasn't lost on Ms. Lana. She softened and smiled gently, and said that legally, there was no issue with it—but that it didn't mean it was the best idea.

For the last eight years of our parenting, we had never, not ever left our kids home alone. Not even for a few minutes. Not to the neighbors house. Not to run to the store. Not even to cross the street to use the swimming pool while they were all sleeping. I absolutely couldn't believe that we could have been doing those things the whole time—I probably would have considered it incredibly neglectful parenting, and yet here we were under investigation because one of our children had died *while under parental supervision.*

After the interviews were completed, we had to take Ms. Lana on a tour of the house. My understanding was that the requirements as far as DSS was concerned were that a house have, 1) Running water, with a functioning bathroom 2) Working electricity. 3) Food in the pantry. 4) A separate sleeping space for each person.

Ever since Ronan was a baby, Brock and I had fully engaged in co-sleeping with our babies until they were around a year old. I was nursing, and the only one doing any night time parenting, and co-sleeping was the easiest way for us to get any sleep. Once we moved out of Brock's parents house, and into the townhome, I decided that there wasn't any reason *not to* just have a big family bedroom. On a whim, I bought two Ikea bunk beds and installed them in the big master bedroom, and then put our king sized bed in between them. Ronan, Ruby and Ryder all slept in the same room as us in their individual bunks, and Rory was still sleeping in bed with us.

We walked into the 'family' bedroom where everyone slept, and I could tell that Ms. Lana was immediately confused. She was young, likely had no children of her own, and had never seen anything like it before. I'll admit, the way I'd chosen to raise and care for my babies was well outside of the mainstream, and I understood that it raised some questions. However, she moved on, having seen and been satisfied that every child had their own sleeping space.

We moved into the bathroom, and she asked us about our dental habits and doctor's visits. She asked us about home-schooling and what that looked like. She asked about laundry and chores and what types of routines we had. All of it felt pretty simple, if a little intrusive, but I didn't mind answering the questions.

As we turned around and returned to the top of the stairs, Ms Lana paused... and then she got very uncomfortable. She looked down at the floor, and her dark cheeks took on a decidedly red cast as she quietly, stumblingly asked, "So...if everyone sleeps in the same bedroom... I mean, if the kids are..." She paused, and tried again, "What I'm trying to ask is... um... where do you... ahem... be intimate?"

Despite all of the worry, and grief and pain of that particular day, and all of the prior questions, her discomfort and her curiosity made me chuckle. I looked at her with a raised eyebrow, and quipped, "Just about everywhere else." Then I laughed and turned around and opened the door to the guest bedroom, where my mother was staying while she was with us and said, "We usually spend time together here after the kids are in bed. But honestly, only being intimate in a bed is wildly unimaginative."

Ms Lana blinked her eyes in shocked surprise a few times, and then looked away, a gentle blush climbing her exquisite cheekbones. She cleared her throat, and then walked back down the stairs and towards the front door.

We stood in front of the entrance to our home, and Ms Lana told us that we were finished with the interview. She thanked us again for our time and patience with her. She apologized once more for having to even be there, and affirmed a second time that it was abundantly clear that we were good people, good parents, and it was entirely unfair that this had happened to us. Her eyes filled with tears as she raised them to mine, possibly the first time she'd made direct eye contact with me that day, and she said, "I'm really, really sorry that Rory died."

As I closed the door behind her, I finally breathed a full sigh of relief. The fear of what that appointment meant had been weighing on me much more than I had recognized. We knew she would be calling back, that we had several required visits before all of it was completely behind us, but it felt like the scariest part was over.

They weren't going to take our other children away.

chapter 18

I woke up to noise in the kitchen. It had been just over a whole week of waking up and remembering that my baby died. It was actually a lovely way to wake up. I didn't spend those first moments in bed forgetting that Rory was gone—I just rolled out of bed and headed down the stairs.

I rounded the corner at the bottom of the stairs into the kitchen, and was snatched up into the biggest bear-hug imaginable. "MAND."

It was Ryan, my middle brother. He was massive, and felt like my childhood, and safety, and home.

I think I knew that everyone was coming, but it wasn't real to me yet. We had told everyone that we were holding a memorial for Rory on February 14th, ten days after his death, and invited everyone we could think of. I didn't really believe they would actually show up.

"I'm so fucking sorry, Mand." My brother's voice made its way up to my ear as he hadn't let go yet. I was struggling a little to breathe, and I started to pull myself out of his grip. Ryan squeezed tighter, and I heard a small snuffle.

He was crying.

Ryan was crying.

I had never before seen my brother cry from sadness. Ryan was built like me—sensitive and loving and tender. But the world treated little boys differently than it did little girls, and he learned early how to shut down and cover up anything that didn't look like joy… or anger.

I forcibly pulled Ryan away from me and looked him in the face. "I'm sorry you have to be here. I'm sorry this hurts so fucking badly. Oh God, Ryan… I'm so glad you came."

He hugged me again, and we both sobbed as we stood there in the front entrance.

There was another knock on the door, and I disengaged from Ryan to reach behind him and open the door.

Standing on my front stoop was a tall, beautiful young woman with a perfect button nose, straight gorgeous teeth, and icy blue eyes. A sprinkle of freckles crossed her face, and she pushed her choppy blond hair out of her face as she looked like she didn't know if she should smile or cry. She held a chubby, gorgeous baby boy in her arms, all cheeks and drool, and fidgeted like she wasn't sure she was in the right place, or if she was supposed to be there at all.

"CRYSTAL!"

I gasped.

Crystal had been my best friend my whole life. Our parents were best friends. Her dad was the best man and my mom and dad's wedding. We grew up sharing dolls, and clothes, and stories, and traumas. Somehow, every time my family moved, Crystal's family was in the same place—either before or after us. We went to the same middle school and survived the same gauntlet of high school. We graduated together and swore we would be best friends forever.

Crystal didn't like Jonas, and we drifted apart while he and I were together—but Crystal LOVED Brock, and our friendship found new footing as we were young mothers together in the era of internet—thousands of miles apart, we texted and video-called and instant messaged each other every single day.

That was until we had a falling out. It's tough to say exactly what it was—maybe our parenting differences, or maybe just the distance. Maybe it was guilt or jealousy or sadness or projection. I will never be sure, but we got into one of our Hallmark Fights on Facebook one afternoon… and never spoke again. I hadn't heard from Crystal since before Rory was born. I didn't think she was my friend anymore, and I had grieved the loss of her like she had died.

Only… she hadn't died. And she was there, like a vision, an apparition, on my doorstep. Looking bashful and contrite, and worried that I was going to turn her away.

In a moment straight out of the movies, I bolted out the door and gripped her to me, and cried and cried and cried. Our tears mingled as she cried too, and then suddenly we were *both* crushed in the massive arms of Ryan—he loved Crystal as well, and was elated to see her.

Over the rest of the day, my oldest brother Adam arrived, and then my dad. I sat in the dining room of my home as my family showed up the night before the memorial of my dead son, and was strangely elated.

Everyone is here, I realized. *Everyone in the world I love is here, and my son is dead.*

Brock's entire family showed up that night as well, and we had the strangest, saddest, most beautiful dinner together—two families mingled in joy and grief, that had not all been together since nine years before, when Brock and I were married at the house on the lake. Judy and Tim were there, and Brady and Thomas. My mom and dad were sitting together at the table, and everyone was talking animatedly. I was so filled with love and still so surprised that everyone had come. I had mistakenly carried this strange disbelief that no one would show up for me, and yet here they were. All of them. And I hadn't even expected them to come.

chapter 19

The morning of February 14th dawned bright and beautiful. It was brisk, but the sun warmed my face when I stepped outside. There was no choice today—I couldn't stay home, safe and cocooned. We had to drive to the funeral home where Rory had been cremated and pick up his ashes.

Brock and I sat in the car, quiet and pensive, on the way to Adam's Funeral Home, a building that we had seen a thousand times and yet had no idea it was there. A quiet, unassuming building behind the bank that we frequented often, next to the Goodwill. For the first time ever, we passed the bank and pulled into a parking spot we had never imagined needing.

We held hands as we walked into the building together. It was somber and beautiful inside. The walls were dark, glossy wood and the air felt warm and welcoming. It was nothing like I would have expected a funeral home to feel; I had assumed it would be cold and sterile and sad. Instead, peaceful music played in the main atrium, and I felt fragile as we navigated the entryway, as though I would break wide open if jostled the wrong way. Brock supported me, holding far more than his fair share of my weight as we walked up to the desk. The gentleman behind the desk was older, and shorter, and soft spoken. His hair was thinning, and he had small, round, wire-rimmed glasses that didn't obstruct the view of his eyes; eyes that held a depth and a knowing that couldn't be mistaken.

"How can I help you?" he asked gently. It took me a moment to find my voice, but I answered, "We are here to pick up our son's…

Rory." My words caught in my throat. I wasn't there to get Rory, I was there to get his ashes, and I couldn't even say it.

The man's eyes immediately filled with deep sorrow and endless compassion. "I'm so, so sorry for your loss," he told us gently. "I will go get him. I'll be right back." The use of Rory's pronoun was profound. I was immediately grateful. My eyes filled with tears at the absurdity of the situation—that I was waiting for someone to bring me my baby in a jar, my baby that I didn't want to be dead, my baby that should be here, and alive, and I should never, ever have to know this building, or this man, or this painful reality.

In that self-same moment, I was struck by the beauty, the unexpected sweetness and sorely welcome tenderness. It was resoundingly clear that this man had known great pain, and yet somehow was willing to face it over and over again.

When he returned, he walked towards us carrying a dark maroon velvet bag. It was so surreal. I couldn't make it make sense in my head. *My baby is in that bag. The body that is my baby is in there. My baby is dead, and burned, and ashes are in that bag that are my baby.* As soon as I saw him, I broke out in fresh sobs. Brock held me and cried into my hair.

Our fucking baby is dead.

The kind man patiently waited for our storm to pass, and then gently handed us our boy, knowing that there was no instance of any reality that could ever exist where this was what we wanted. Knowing that this was the worst of all possible outcomes, and that we would never, ever choose it, and yet we had to accept it.

I smiled wanly at him and said, "Thank you. For helping us, and for your kindness." I told him that everyone we had dealt with from their place of business had been so wonderful, and for some reason, to me, it was kind of surprising. He gently informed us that most people enter into the funeral business because of their own loss, and because of how much it meant to them to be treated well—his experience was the death of his wife, and the way he was cared for changed his life.

That was a formative moment for me—seeing and feeling how being loved well during the lowest, most painful moment of your life could make a new foundation for how you could choose to *be with* people in the future. That it was possible to be loved *so well* during loss that you could spread that love forward and outward and beyond without reservation, already knowing the difference it could make because you remember what it did for you. That, to me, seemed like the most beautiful expansion—a fractal, a crystalline explosion of compassion and passion and love.

We turned to leave through the strangely out-of-place automatic doors, and walked back to our car. I sat down in my seat, and Brock closed the car door for me, and then got in the driver's seat next to me. We sat there in silence for a moment, and then I opened the velvet bag. I pulled out Rory's tiny, blue marbled stone urn. It was so beautiful. It took my breath away. Squat, short and round and all soft curves and edges. "Rory Kai Allender" was inscribed on it, with the dates of his life underneath. Then, below that, "I'm sorry, I love you, Thank you, Please Forgive Me." I was immediately pulled under again, awash in the surreality of it again, and sobbed, deeply wrenched open again, that this beautiful urn was all that was left of our sweet, perfect, soft, round little boy.

We attended the memorial for our son later that night. Not only had my entire family come into town for the event, but I was completely surrounded by everyone that I loved. All of my friends and important people. Everyone that mattered in Brock's life showed up as well. It was so painfully beautiful; colors and candles and thousands of pictures of Rory strung up everywhere. All of the images I had ever taken of him and posted on instagram were printed out in sweet little squares of wonder. Everywhere I looked, he was there. He was there in the smiles, and there in the laughter, and there in the tears.

We had asked Steve, a dear pastor friend of ours, to speak at the memorial. A few days before the event, he invited us over to their home and read to us what he had written. Brock and I were sitting in his kitchen, not completely in grief or suffering, and quite

glad to be out of the house and not in public. We were chatting
with Steve and his wife, and talking about things that had nothing
to do with our child dying, or what was coming up. Eventually,
we had to get down to business, and Steve pulled out four pieces
of paper. He looked me directly in the eye, and said, "I'm so sorry
that we even have to do this. I'm so sorry I had to write this. I'm
so sorry that Rory isn't here."

My eyes immediately filled with tears, and I listened to him as
he spoke deeply and beautifully about the nature of life, and when
it ends. It was perfect, and beautiful, and heartbreaking.

When Steve got up at Rory's memorial, I didn't hear him
there. I had already heard his eulogy, and I couldn't put myself in
the space to attend to it. Instead, I looked around the table, around
the room. Instead, I waited to see the impact his words had on
everyone else. They had already torn me wide open. My eyes fell
on my mother, and witnessed her tears. My heart opened towards
her, the first time I'd seen her cry since arriving. She showed up
when asked, and was as solid as a rock—a stable port in the storm.

Then I looked at my brothers, just barely holding back their
sorrow, and I was immediately so thankful they were there. Willing
to be there for me, and willing to look at something so hard and
tender. I looked over at Brock, who was openly weeping, and took
his hand. We were in the thick of it together at that exact moment.
I glanced quickly around the room and saw eyes brimming over
everywhere that I turned.

Finally, I turned my head and looked at my father. I had been
avoiding looking at him. I knew that he didn't really want to come
to the memorial—I knew that he really didn't want to come at all.
I had been angry and resentful as my mother told me that he was
resisting the trip, and asking her to come home instead. I thought
he was being selfish. But in that moment, I didn't just see my father.
I gasped as I looked at my dad and saw an agony on his face that
I had not seen before, that I had not remembered in my own pain.

It wasn't until that exact moment that I recalled that my father
had walked this path already. My dad's little sister, Holly, died when

he was fourteen years old. I had known. I had always known. My family had told me the story of Holly. I knew that his baby sister had cancer, and I knew that she died in the hospital after months and years of treatment, and I knew that her death tore his family apart. I knew all of that, and yet I didn't *know* it. Until that moment, I had never really known it.

My eyes swelled with compassion and empathy and tears flowed anew as I looked at my dear, quiet, sweet, stern father and saw pain pouring out of him that had nothing to do with the death of my child. It truly wasn't until that very moment that I realized my father had gone through exactly what my children were going through. More than that, I could only imagine that the re-opening of those decades old wounds must have been agony.

Eventually, the memorial ended, as all things must. I was sad to leave, as though another door to the life that Rory had lived was closing behind us—the memorial was over and he was truly gone.

We left the church and headed home, drained to the extreme. Exhausted. Completely spent. Another major milestone was behind us, but it was another step farther away from the moments when Rory was alive, and it felt like we were leaving him behind too. I wept all the way back.

But once we arrived there, our home was filled with the most glorious light. Everyone was there—all of my family, and all of Brock's family, and our closest friends and loved ones—we were all still together and it was unreal. It was magical. We laughed and smiled and felt gratitude and revelled in the joy of togetherness, despite the soft blanket of sorrow. There was a part of me that felt guilty for being happy; for feeling so full of love and gratitude in the midst of my deep longing and loss. But it was so necessary: the laughing, and the companionship, and the stories, and the heart.

Unfortunately, behind all of that joy was the knowledge that it had to end. The very next day, my father would leave… and it was just the beginning. The beginning of the leaving. Everyone had come, but that also meant that they had to go again.

chapter 20

As friends and family members began to depart, I started to realize that there was one inescapable truth; we had no choice but to eventually come back to life. That is a hard request of a grieving person, an unfair ask. It's so much. But the reality is that children still need to be fed, and the house still needs to be cleaned, and life... it really is meant to be lived.

Dad was the first to leave. He came for just over 24 hours and had absolutely no trouble leaving. I had wanted him to stay longer, but I understood and had compassion for the fact that my pain was a deep, uncomfortable echo of his own. While I think it's possible he wasn't aware of what was going on for him, it was readily apparent to me and I had no desire to see him suffer.

Next to go was my biggest brother, Adam; he was a police officer and had just a few days of leave that he had used to come love and support me, and that felt so wonderful. I hadn't even expected him to come, and was so thankful that he had.

Then it was Crystal's turn to leave; she had a farm to get back to, and also her whole entire life in Canada. Despite the sorrow and pain, I was deliriously happy to get that time with her. We had all fallen in love with her darling son, Gus, and were sad that he was leaving too. I cried and kissed her firmly on the cheek and we promised that we wouldn't let it be years before we saw each other again. We promised that we'd never let a foolish fight tear us apart again—it just mattered too much.

Ryan left next. Life with Ryan in it was so full—so rich and so beautiful. He loved so hard, and cared so much, and gave so often. He did all sorts of shit with my kids that only an uncle would do, and in those particular moments, I had absolutely no capacity to even begin to try. I had never been so grateful for the brothers that had been mine my whole entire life, and had never truly seen how much they loved and cherished me. It was astonishing.

Last to leave was my mama, and that goodbye was the hardest.

I didn't want her to go. There was a whole lot of pain and loneliness and unfamiliar territory in front of me, and doing it without my mom there to clean and cook and help felt awful. Big and huge and scary and terrible. But I knew that coming back to life meant coming back to all parts of it, and I knew that my mama had to go back to her own life as well.

Life is meant to be lived.

I wouldn't let anyone else drive her to the airport. Even though I hadn't driven since Rory died, I was adamant that it would be me. She and I loaded into the car and drove the 35 minutes to the airport, chatting lightly and smiling gently as we pretended that everything was fine—this was just another day together.

I parked in the short-term lot. I wasn't willing to just drop her off at departures. There was no way I could let her get out of the car, wave from the driver's seat, and drive off. Not a chance. So I parked, and we walked in together. I absolutely knew I was prolonging the separation like a toddler stalling bedtime, but I didn't care. I was going to take every single second that I could get.

Mom was always strict about airport times, and we arrived at the ticket counter a full three hours before her plane was scheduled to leave. The lines at security weren't all that long, so I asked mom if she wanted to grab a coffee before she left for good. My mother is literally always down for coffee, so we got two large black coffees, (that I added a crapload of milk to,) and she sipped hers black as coal. Minutes passed as we sat on a bench, facing each other and knees touching, as close a seat as we could find to the security checkpoint.

For a while, we kept playing the 'you're not really leaving game,' but eventually, my eyes misted and I said, "Mom. I just have to tell you…" I wept gently as I stumbled through the words, "… I'm so, so glad you came. I needed you so badly. And you didn't have to come, but it means so fucking much that you did."

Mom's eyes glistened as well, and she grabbed my hand as I continued, "You have always been so wonderful, mom. So wonderful. I can't even begin to tell you how lucky I am that you are my mom. I love you so, so fucking much. And I'm so goddamn sorry for all of this pain."

Mom pulled her hand out of mine, and set her coffee down and wrapped her arms around me. She held me tightly, and wiped away her own tears, whispering her own apology, "I'm so so sorry that Rory died, Mand. I'm so sorry I have to leave. I would stay if I could. I wish I could."

We both knew that there was no *right* to this, no easy way to do it. It was just all hard. She pulled away from me, holding me back out at arms length, and whispered, "I promise it won't be years before I see you again. I promise I'll come back. Oh babe, I promise. Cross my heart. Hope to die."

And eventually, despite my stalling and hoping and wishing, it really was time. There were no more minutes to waste, no more excuses to make. There was no other choice but to say goodbye. She stood, and I stood, and we wrapped our arms around each other again and held on for dear life. I deeply breathed her in, and thanked her once again, and then let go. She kissed my cheek soundly, said "I love you," firmly, and turned and walked away.

I numbly returned to my car, and sat there, taking in the enormity of what had come and gone. It was impossible to ignore: the immediate grief period, the dying time was at an end. I didn't know what came next. I didn't know where to go from there. All I knew was that I was still alive, and I knew I *must* be alive because it hurt so fucking badly.

When I got home, I came into the house and sat at the table that suddenly felt abandoned. Desperately empty. Like a mausoleum. The space that had been filled with people, not ever empty for the last fifteen days, was completely desolate. It was just me, and the completed jigsaw puzzle that rested in the center of the table.

The grief puzzle.

Every person that came into my home had sat around that puzzle with me at some point, and each person that visited glanced over it as it was constructed, adding a piece or two here and there. The image was deeply rich and complex, and the build was challenging. Once it was finally finished, several days later, I looked over it and found myself so grateful for it; the puzzle, and what it represented.

The thing is, humans are relational creatures. To my knowledge, we spend the majority of our time trying to figure out how to relate to other humans—both how to understand someone else's experience, and how to communicate our own. We have words, and body language, and art, and energy; music and film and written word.

When a person goes through something terrible, that person may spend an awful lot of time and effort trying to share, to explain the reality of their terrible experience with others. It often feels like a foolish endeavor, because unless someone has gone through that same terrible event, no descriptor will completely encapsulate what the experience was; and conversely, if someone *has* been through that event, they don't need someone to explain it. They already know.

Yet we persist.

In this persistence, what comes up are a whole host of cliches—simple, familiar comparisons that boil down the complexity of the reality into something that's easy to understand and digest, and are destined to fall woefully short.

Allow me to contribute my own cliche to the mix.

When Rory died, my life shattered apart into thousands of pieces. I was lost. Who I was and what I had understood life to be was completely obliterated, like a jigsaw puzzle thrown into a box and wildly shaken. I no longer had a handle on how to exist—how to eat, how to feel, how to talk, how to react. I forgot how to take care of my body, and was absolutely unavailable to care for my living kids. I didn't know how to be a wife to my husband, and I certainly lost the ability to be a friend (good or otherwise).

It didn't occur to me, when I bought the grief puzzle, that I was purchasing the perfect representation of my life after loss, nor that it would exactly mirror the process of putting myself back together. When I originally dumped the cardboard tumult of colors and shapes and images out onto the table, I couldn't help but feel a momentary flash of solidarity.

Same, puzzle. Same.

Just like the puzzle, as each day that went by, a bit of myself got put together again. First the edge pieces—re-assembling how to live in a human body. How to eat, how to sleep, how to get clean and dress. How to enjoy food again. Friends and folks showed up with meals and gifts and clothes, and each of them put a few pieces of the puzzle into place—both on the kitchen table, and within my soul. As the frame of the puzzle was built, so was the scaffold of the life that I was reassembling and didn't yet recognize. At the time, there was just too much left undone.

Day by day, slowly, and requiring intense patience, parts of the puzzle filled in. A corner over here, beautiful and resplendent with colors and imagery; my ability to sit with my children and hear their thoughts and feelings without becoming overwhelmed.

There, a giant mass of spirals and towers that came together; my marriage feeling solid and safe again. Piece after piece fell perfectly into place, and without fail, the whole picture started to appear. It was there all along, amidst the tumult and turmoil.

And that day, after my mother flew away, I was left with a completed puzzle all brought back together, order to the chaos, with nothing else to wonder but, *'what next'?* What do we do with it?

Do we keep it here on the table? Do we take it back apart again? Glue it? Frame it? Give it away??

As I sat at the table and looked down at the magnificent design in front of me, I was completely overcome with awe: each and every single soul that came into our home, each person that had poured love and healing and help upon us, each hand had touched the cardboard edges and painted surface. It wasn't lost on me that the puzzle was a powerful, absolutely perfect symbol of those days in our lives; reassembling our broken existence, piecing ourselves back together, finding ourselves whole, and filled up with love, and... with absolutely no idea how to move forward without our one, perfect, tiny missing piece.

chapter 21

There was no way for me to know what coming back to life would look like. I hadn't been given a road map. All I could do was feel it out, and trust that my tender heart and my intuition would guide me.

My kids were beyond ready to return to some semblance of normal. We had been homeschooling for the last several years, and had joined a little weekly co-op for friends and socialization. We had missed several weeks in a row, and it felt like time to go back.

The group was lovely and large and full of other women that were used to care-giving and sharing the load. I figured that it would be gentle to ease back in, and have others help with my children. They also all knew the story, so I wouldn't have to guard myself or explain what had happened to anyone.

Three weeks since Rory's death, and our first day back, my kids all tumbled out of the car in a flurry of excitement. I was moving more slowly, not entirely sure I was ready to be there. "Don't run inside," I shouted at the backs disappearing ahead of me, and shuffled into the space a few moments after the door had already swung shut. I glanced around the room and made sure I had eyes on each of my children, and then took a deep breath. I could see all three of them. I didn't have to worry. I set my things down on a couch in the corner, and immediately started to help with the process of setting up the co-op space: moving tables out of the way, sliding chairs around, and assembling stations for classes.

I watched for a moment as several children tried to slide a

glass-topped coffee-table out of the way, and assessed that they were struggling far more than they needed to. The table was round, and could just be flipped up on its side and rolled into place. Simple. "Here, let me help," I said as I walked over and placed my hands under the lip of the table, and flipped it onto the edge without a second thought.

My eyes widened in surprise as the circular glass set into the center of the table pitched forward out of its seat, and fell as though in slow motion to shatter on the floor.

The sound was tremendous. Glass shards broke into millions of tiny fragments, crystals that slid across the floor and threw rainbows on the walls. I stood there, frozen, utterly perplexed and completely unable to comprehend what had just happened.

The whole world paused for just a moment, and then the other ladies rushed in—swooped to my rescue. Someone removed the table from my hands, and someone else began sweeping. Another mom immediately began shoo-ing the kids away so no one would be cut on the multitude of broken glass. Yet another mom gently guided me by the elbow to the nearest chair, where I collapsed into tears yet again.

I shouldn't be here. I can't function. I'm not ready for this.

I had buried my eyes in my hands, and couldn't look up. I didn't want to. I didn't want to meet any of the eyes surrounding me. I was terrified of what I was sure I would find there, behind the gentle frowns and concerned eyebrows: I couldn't bear to see the pity.

Pity is like empathy—close, but not quite. It's like empathy's nasty cousin that is sure that 'whatever is happening to you could never possibly happen to me. I wouldn't let it.'

The mother beside me gave me a gentle hug and said quietly, "You don't have to stay. You can go home. We'll take care of the kids." I nodded, snuffled, and wiped my nose on my sleeve as I stood up and tried not to make eye contact with anyone else in the room. *No pity. No thank you.*

I started towards the door, and then realized I should probably tell my kids that I was leaving. I paused and turned around, back towards the entire room, and guarded my heart as I looked out for my children. But, gosh, I couldn't believe it. All of the eyes looking back at me were filled with so much love and compassion and empathy. Not a frown. Not a smirk. Not a knowing glance nor a spiteful shrug. I didn't spy a single speck of pity. My eyes immediately filled with tears again as I realized that my people were caring for me, truly caring, and I had had nothing to fear. Not alone. Not pitied. Loved, and held, and cared for.

I found my children and told them that I was going home, but that they could stay. No one was bothered by the prospect, as I had interrupted their playing, so I grabbed my things and went back home again.

Continuing to *come back to life* was a long, drawn out struggle for me. I pendulated back and forth between staying home because it was safe and easy; and going out, being with others, seeing friends because that was life. I knew that my children weren't deeply grieving, and some part of me knew that I also had to let my children live. Not just exist. Not just hole up at home because it was safer, easier for me.

They had to *live*.

It would have been so easy to grip harder, grasp fiercer, hold tighter on to them. It would have been so easy to immediately change the way we parented, as though the freely loving way we had been doing it before was wrong. But, closing in and clenching down didn't feel right. It didn't feel like living. We knew that we wanted our kids to still be allowed to play, to explore, and to *swim*. We knew that there were no guarantees, and that the chance always existed that we could lose someone else. We knew that, but we wanted to live through it and beyond it.

It didn't stop the knee-jerk terror, though. Maybe you know the one I'm talking about. It's the one where you fear the absolute worst, and you feel it right in the center of your being. It is the "*surely not*". And since one of my knee-jerk terrors had come true, I felt like I was primed and deeply helpless to its power. I lived for months and months with repeat knee-jerk terror. Every time

I heard a loud thump, or a squeal. Every time I backed out of a parking lot, I had to stop and get out of my car and make sure there wasn't a child behind it. The intrusive thoughts and the gut-drops were constant.

Not again. Please, not again.

One afternoon, Ryder was taking a bath, and when Ryder bathes, he bathes LOUD. He splashes, and thuds, and jumps around. Without a doubt, there would be more water on the floor than in the tub when he finished. I knew that, and it was still worth the relative peace and quiet having him entertained for a handful of minutes.

Because he was in the bath, and more than old enough to be trusted there, I was puttering around, folding laundry and putting it away when I realized that it was totally silent.

Oh god, no.

I knee-jerked into terror, and bolted up the stairs into the bathroom as fast as I could humanly move.

Not again. Please not again.

Ryder was laying face down in the tub, head in the water, and peachy little booty floating above the surface, but he was perfectly still. "RYDER!" I shrieked, my heart shattered with fear.

Not again. Not again.

Ryder popped up joyfully out of the tub, giant-ass-grin plastered across his face as the water streamed down.

"Didja see me, mama? Didja see how long I held my bwef??"

Oh, my child. I did. But you scared me almost all the way to death.

About a week later, I realized that we still had plane tickets for a trip to Canada that was supposed to be so my family could meet Ryder and Rory. We'd had two whole entire children since the last time I was home. I'd purchased the tickets in November. A few days before Rory died, we had gone out and gotten passport photos taken, and I still consider those some of my greatest treasures.

But passport photos are not enough, and I had to file for actual passports for the kids to travel. I made an appointment for a certain day, and gathered all of my papers, and had everything set out and ready for when it was time to go. I knew that I wasn't functioning with normal capacity—there is something about grief that lowers or maybe dulls the acuity of everything, including thought. But I was doing my best. I got in my car to go to the appointment, and firmed up my resolve; going into public was still hard. I made it to the building on time, and found parking, and even managed to find the right entrance (all very high level stress points for me.). I walked into the building and navigated my way to the Passport Office.

I was proud of myself as I got to my appointment on time, sat at the desk with the passport lady, and handed her all of our completed paperwork. I explained that we were going to Canada in a few weeks, and that everything should be in order. She shuffled quickly through my papers, and looked up at me with impatience and irritation. "You don't have their birth certificates here," she snapped brusquely.

My eyes widened in shock at her rough tone, but I remembered tucking them into my wallet. "They're right here, just…" I patted around and looked more and more frantically as I realized that my wallet *was not* present and accounted for. I slumped in my chair and felt the prickle of tears as the woman sighed and said, "So, this was an entire waste of time. You'll have to leave and make another appointment."

It felt like a punch in the gut. I knew that she didn't know that my son had just died, nor that I was just barely functioning in general, but I also felt that her treatment of me was below the basic level of compassion for even fully operational humans. Tears freely poured down my face as I stumbled out of the passport office and navigated my way back to my car. I sat in the parking deck, head on my arms, and sobbed and sobbed and sobbed.

Coming back to life meant that sometimes I was doing okay—like I was living and pretending to function in the world where my baby was already gone. Doing okay meant I was pretending well. Sometimes, I was just Mandy, and I was married to a wonderful husband, and we had three gorgeous kiddos, and our baby died.

But sometimes? Sometimes I was *OH MY GOD MY BABY DIED*.

I never knew what was going to trip me into one of those moments. Maybe it was a song on the radio. Often it was finding a picture that I hadn't seen in a while. Occasionally it was a glimpse of a stranger, a little boy with brown skin and brown hair. Perhaps it was a particularly beautiful sky.

And one specific time, it looked like standing in line at Panera Bread, waiting to order my food, when the sweet older lady in front of me smiled gently and said, "I love your shoes.' It looked like glancing down at the shoes on my feet, and realizing that they weren't my shoes—they belonged to Judy, because my shoes were soaking wet from jumping in the lake to rescue my baby, and I hadn't yet been able to return to the lake house to get them, and *OH MY GOD MY BABY DIED*.

Life felt like a minefield. I never knew which moments I would tolerate well, and which would cause me to smile gently, eyes quickly filling, and turn around and immediately leave the restaurant because *oh my god my baby died.*

chapter 22

One month after Rory died, Brock and I walked into a tattoo studio called Haylo's Healing Lounge for a consultation about a memorial tattoo. I was gifted a certificate for a deposit by a loving friend, and God, I was so not ready to get a tattoo. I mean, yes, I wanted a tattoo to commemorate my son. Yes, I wanted to put the memory of his life into my skin. Yes, I wanted it to be somewhere I could see it. Yes, I wanted people to ask me about it. All the time. Getting a tattoo in honor of Rory was one of the best ideas I had ever heard. Because all of those things were true, I had to be ready. It was one of the most worthy things I could imagine. But I didn't want it, and I wasn't ready for it yet. I still just wanted my son.

For days and days before the consultation, I sat and thought about what I would have tattooed. I decided that I wanted his name in big, black, bold letters down my forearm. Then I thought about adding other words around him in colors, making something like a tartan of plaid or a patchwork quilt of other important things. Words that described him. 'Sweet' and 'Peaceful' and 'Mischievous' and 'Clever'. That seemed perfect. I had nailed it down, and I could even picture it in my mind. I knew exactly what to ask the artist for.

We were guided into the large, underground studio and asked to sit down on a little purple couch. Brock was close beside me, and we introduced ourselves to Hayley, our artist, as she walked up and sat down across from us. She was of medium height and a slight build, with long brown hair that ended in beautiful, colorfully decorated dreadlocks. She was completely covered, all of the skin that I could see save her face, in the most intricate, delicate, colorful, detailed and expressive tattoos I had ever seen. I didn't even know that tattoos could look like that. They took my breath away.

We told her the story of Rory, and how I wanted something on my skin and in my skin that could never be removed. It was my first ever tattoo. I explained to her what I wanted, proud to have walked in with a finished concept that felt so complete and so cool.

Hayley listened compassionately and doodled some ideas while we were talking. Then she looked up at me and smiled gently and asked, "How married are you to that idea?"

I thought about it for a second, my eyes widened in mild surprise, and I shrugged. I realized that I actually didn't have any other ideas, but also that I hadn't considered any other options. After seeing the breathtaking art covering her body, I was prompted to ask, "What do you have in mind?"

Hayley looked down at her papers and began asking gentle questions. She was soft spoken and unassuming, and felt safe and compassionate. She asked about my other kids, and what they were like. Her eyes flicked up to me and back down to her sketch pad as she listened. She asked about Rory; about what his name meant, and about his personality, what I loved about him and what I missed about him. She asked about things I was passionate about, and what my dreams were. She asked me a whole litany of questions and I couldn't even begin to imagine what she was thinking, what direction she was heading or what she could possibly be sketching as we talked. Tears gently poured down my face as I responded.

Finally, after fifteen or twenty minutes of chatting to what seemed like idle doodle, Hayley turned the paper around and showed me the sketch. "What do you think of this?"

I gasped, and then immediately sobbed. It was beautiful. Hard to describe in words, more of an artistic representation of what pain and joy and the entirety of a human existence could look like.

It had a beautiful aqua double-swirl for Rory, and sweet, smooth round river stones for Ronan. Ruby was represented as pink and purple air, and Ryder's powerful existence was encompassed in flames and sparks along the outside edge. Bubbles along the inner curve, one for each month of Rory's beautiful life. Stars at the top, including the Pegasus constellation, where the Rory Kai star lives. I immediately knew that that image needed to be tattooed on my body. It was absolutely perfect.

On March 22nd, three weeks later, I sat down in Hayley's chair and had the first session of what would eventually become a full-sleeve memorial tattoo. My first session lasted five hours, and it was intensely painful. Worse than I expected, and yet somehow satisfying. I needed to feel that physical pain. A few hours in, I told Hayley that the actual wounding of my skin felt like the most accurate possible representation for the spiritual and emotional pain that I had been carrying since Rory died. I was so grateful for the experience, even as I was hurting through it.

In five hours of pain and commiseration, you get to learn a little bit about the person you've chosen to do your art, if you're open to it. I asked Hayley a whole litany of questions about herself and her life, and found myself falling deeply into love and compassion for her in return. Hayley had lost both her mother and her father, and had found tattooing as a helpful and healing modality. It was why she had opened up her studio, the healing lounge. It was why she understood my grief so well, and didn't look away.

At the end of my session, I looked down with pride at my new permanent art, and cried again. I was so in love with it. It was so much more than I could have dreamed it would be. I hugged Hayley and explained that even thought I knew she was using tiny needles to shove ink into my skin, it felt very much like what she was doing was reaching in and pulling out my pain and hurt and soul and beauty and love… and putting it on the surface, laying it out plainly for the world to see. What a gift that was.

And the biggest motherfucker of the whole entire thing was that I was so excited to have a brand new, beautiful, painful tattoo in honor of my dead son… and I would have given every ounce of that art and moment and thrill and excitement up to have just one more second, one more moment of time with him instead.

$$\odot$$

Many, many nights, I just laid in bed and tried not to think. Tried not to breathe. Tried not to be. I wished so badly for all of the grief and pain to stop, and there it was. So instead, I would turn over and open my phone. I would spend hours and hours looking at pictures and videos of Rory, and just let myself pour out whatever grief was there to be let go of. Sometimes I smiled. Sometimes I laughed. Sometimes I begged. But mostly, I cried until I was so tired that my eyes could no longer stay open, and I would finally collapse into exhaustion.

I just kept not taking the pills, and I just kept laying there, trying to heal. One night, I'm not even sure when, but weeks after Rory's death, I was laying in bed as usual. Instead of opening my phone, however, my thoughts just kept going back to the day at the lake. It was the one place I tried to avoid above all others. The terror place. Over and over, my heart would start racing and my breath would constrict in my lungs as my mind wandered back there again, no matter how hard I tried not to. Back to the lake house. Back to the day.

I fought it, but I was hijacked. It didn't matter what else I tried to think about, I couldn't go anywhere or do anything when I was stuck in the flashback. I felt it in my body, in my breath, in my heart. My legs ached with the cold. My eyes burned with the tears. It all felt real and true and crystal clear, as though it were happening again—still—in that moment. I was stuck.

Hours passed, hours stuck in the traumatic memory that was locked in my body. I was laying there, exhausted from sobbing and trying to free myself, when I finally, suddenly, realized where the terror was. The terror wasn't that he died—I had already lived through that. I had survived his death already. It wasn't the outcome that was locking me in.

The terror was in the *not knowing* if Rory would be okay. The reason those moments were so horrifying as I was reliving them was because I was feeling the fear of *not knowing*. The aching cold. The burning tears. My body was replaying the not knowing, the moments where I was afraid he would be dead.

But… I didn't have to be afraid of that.

I know how this ends, I realized with a strange lightness, *I know that he dies*.

I took several long, deep breaths and calmed my racing heart down. I slowed my mind, and made a decision. I could feel that the fear of *not knowing* was trapped in my body. And I thought I knew how I could let it out.

I put my left hand on my heart, and my right hand on my belly, and intentionally walked back into the memory of the day. I purposefully pulled up the fear of wondering why I couldn't hear the kids. Almost immediately, my heart started pounding and I felt the worry rise into my throat. This time, though, I had a plan. I felt my body start to tense and shake, and instead of fighting it, instead of trying to STOP feeling it, I took several deep breaths, and told myself, "It's okay, Mandy. You know how this ends. You know that he dies."

I said it over and over until my heart beat slowed, and my muscles released, and I could breathe normally again. And then I kept going. I stepped forward through each of the memories that brought me into the terror place.

Running into the house.

Pause, breathe, remember.

Yelling up to the garage.

Pause, breathe, remember.

The moment where I started down to the water.

Pause. Breathe. Remember.

Over and over.

You know how this ends. You know that he dies.

The moment where I found him; the moment the EMS took over; the moment we arrived at the hospital; the moment that they turned off the machines and pulled out all of the tubes.

Lovingly, gently, I told myself over and over, "You don't have to do this anymore. He died. You only had to do that one time. You don't have to be afraid anymore."

By the end of it, I had walked with myself and slowed my heart and reminded my soul that I was free from the fear of losing him from the beginning until the entire end.

And I was free.

I also realized, as I had forged slowly and intentionally through that terror, that I had felt it before. It was there, present, at the moment of his birth. That same deep, dark fear. I felt it when he was born into water, and I felt it as he left in the water. I closed my eyes in gratitude, exhausted, and thanked Rory for sending me that gift—the knowledge that I didn't have to carry that *not-knowing* forever. I had moved through it, and I fell deeply, peacefully asleep.

chapter 23

"How are the kids?"

I was still their mother. And Brock was still their father. And the absolute truth of the matter is, kids don't really care enough about anyone but themselves enough to understand grief, or deep sadness, or why things aren't the way they used to be. I'm sure they would have if they could have—but the child brain just doesn't have the capacity. Really, as children should, they still just wanted love, attention, and snacks, regardless of their parents' ability to provide those things.

Having to meet the needs of my kids in the immediacy of grief was one of the hardest things I've ever done; but also, probably, one of the most vital. They still needed me, and I still loved them. Without that anchor, I may have drifted completely away.

We were very open and honest with our kids about what was going on in their lives—they knew that their brother had died, and also a very basic, simple explanation of what that meant. That his heart was no longer beating, and that his lungs were no longer breathing, and that meant he wasn't alive anymore. We followed the time tested advice to only answer the exact question we were asked, without going into deep explanations, and to stop if they seemed satisfied with the answer. It worked very well. We had children's books about death, and about where people go when they die, and what it looks like to feel sadness and grief and all of that.

In the days surrounding his death, my children didn't really cry because Rory was gone. As a matter of fact, they still blamed all of the messes we found in the kitchen on Rory. It wasn't until then that I realized that maybe they had been using him as a scapegoat all along. *Turds.* Anyway, we talked about Rory every day. We said that we missed him every night. When I cried, I explained to the kids that I would probably cry forever. It didn't really seem to bother them. They took it all in stride.

Brock and I understood that their lack of grief wasn't selfishness or sociopathy—just a very limited ability to understand the depth of experience for anyone other than themselves. We also knew that it would morph and shift and change as they got older; that likely we would have to explain things again and again as they went through different developmental stages in their lives.

What we instead found challenging was to try to figure out, at any given point, what might be the cause for any weird emotions or behavioral disruptions.

Is this because you are 4? Or because your brother died?

Are you doing this because you need attention? Or because your mom cries every day?

Could you be getting sick? Or are you processing emotions that you can't yet name?

Truthfully, the answer was most likely 'both' in each scenario. Our only option, at every juncture, was to do the best we could. That's it. Full stop.

Sometimes the best that I could was wonderful, and I was able to sit and talk and explain and laugh and cry and play. And sometimes, all I was able to say was, "Sorry guys. Mom can't right now," and then give myself permission to just not.

We stayed at the co-op and continued 'homeschooling' for the rest of that school year. I have homeschooling in quotation marks because I honestly didn't have anything to give, and a lot of our homeschooling looked like reading together on the couch—passing the book around to kids who could read—and then letting the kids play math apps on tablets. I loved having them around, and was grateful for the opportunity to spend time with them—and I HAD loved actively homeschooling them in the past. But that wasn't where I was in my life or in my headspace. Eventually, I realized that I wasn't really giving them anything worthwhile, and the kindest thing I could do for both my kids and myself was to enroll them into a school, and allow someone else to help. My therapist lovingly reminded me that teachers become teachers mostly because they love kids, and they love teaching—and that school can be a part of 'the village'.

I entered my kids into the lottery to attend an outdoor-heavy, social-emotionally focused nature school that was just 15 minutes away from our home, and was absolutely flabbergasted when both Ruby and Ronan's names were drawn in the lottery. The chances were astronomical, and I took it as a sign that I was making the right choice for my bright, beautiful, smart, inquisitive children. We toured the school, and they were so excited. Ryder wasn't old enough for kindergarten yet, but he was massively envious that 'the guys' were going to get to go to this incredible outdoor nature wonderland.

I felt a ton of guilt as I packed lunches and filled backpacks and dressed my kids up for their first day of school... and heard a tiny voice in my head, which sounded remarkably like my therapist's whispered to me, 'Let the village help.'

I dropped my two older kids off at school, and suddenly my car felt empty. More empty than before. Ryder was at home with Brock, who was working from home. I was entirely alone. It had been months since Rory died, and every minute of every day, I wanted to *feel him*. I wanted to know that he was still around me, that he still existed. I looked for him everywhere. I knew that other people had seen and felt their loved ones in 'signs'. There were all the typical ones, like cardinals, or rainbows, or bees, or butterflies. Before losing Rory, I had always been curious about what it was that made something a *sign*; what other people had felt or seen or heard that made them connect that specific thing to their lost person.

Gosh, I wanted it so badly. So desperately. I wanted to see Rory in the bees, and in the clouds, and in the wind. I had still not ever developed any specific faith nor joined any kind of religion. I didn't have a concrete belief in the afterlife; but I DID believe in Rory. Some part of me just knew that he still existed, and he was *somewhere*. Every day, I looked, constantly, for anything unusual, anything out of place, anything sweet or startling to call a sign from my son. I craved it so powerfully and the absence of it felt so empty. Every time I saw something unusual, I would ask out loud, 'Is that you, babe?' I wanted to believe *any* of them were signs, and I just didn't. I tried to convince myself he was in all of them, but there was nothing special. Nothing visceral. Nothing felt like a touch from him.

It hurt so much. Like I didn't deserve a sign, or I didn't have enough faith to see him or feel him. It was sad, and lonely, and made me think that maybe he *was* just gone for good. That there was no other place. I was completely wrong. I wasn't going to get anything. I started to accept it, even though it held the touches of darkness at its fringes.

At the end of that school day, I climbed back into the car to pick up my kids, and spoke to Rory out loud, as had become my habit—somehow it was always easiest to talk to him when I was alone in the car.

"Hey bud. I miss you. I love you."

I pulled out onto the road, and continued, as tears filled my eyes. "I'm so sorry that this is so hard for me. I'm sorry that I'm sad all the time. I'm trying to find joy. To be happy that I'm alive, and you're not."

My words caught in the back of my throat as grief threatened to overwhelm. My pitch got higher, and my words came faster as the desperation I was feeling took hold.

"I just... Rory... I need to know that you're still there. I need a sign. I'm losing faith... It hurts too badly. I just... I need something. Please."

I could feel the heaviness inside my chest as I drove; feeling nothing and hearing nothing and allowing my heart to break at the emptiness. I took a deep breath, on the verge of despair, and held it as I eased my car around a long gentle turn in the road.

At that exact moment, I turned my head and looked out the window. Across a brief flash of fields that was only visible at that exact spot on the road, my held breath burst from my lungs as my eyes caught sight of the biggest, brightest, most beautiful rainbow that I had ever seen. A rainbow that filled an entire valley. A rainbow that I could only have seen from that angle, on that road, at that specific moment. A rainbow that I could have entirely missed, had I only not turned my head. I burst out laughing, a full belly laugh mingled with immediate tears as I said, "Oh buddy. Oh sweet boy. I see you. Thank you. Thank you my Rory." My heart exploded with light and color and love and wonder.

He is not gone. He is not gone. He is just different.

From that moment forward, I never doubted if a sign was mine, or meant for me, nor whether or not they were from my boy. If it were my choice, if I got to decide whether or not something was a miracle, I decided to see that *everything* was a miracle. I made the choice, I was surrounded by miracles, and I saw signs meant for me everywhere.

Eventually, a swirl became the most often seen Rory-sign, and every single one felt like magic. I would find one walking across the street, just randomly, a little metal swirl-shaped paperclip on the ground. Or a bottle cap at the park would have a blue swirl on the top. Or we'd be heading in to get groceries, and a leaf would fall to the ground and land in a perfect spiral. My heart filled with love and joy at each one. Every time my kids saw one, they would yell, "Rory! Mom, look! It's a Rory Swirl!"

But those weren't the only signs. Every now and then, when I was washing dishes, and I would pick up the dish soap bottle, a little puff of tiny, brilliant, perfect bubbles would spout into the air. Always, they would float up, delightfully, and always there would be one bubble that would float higher, and last longer than every other bubble. It didn't and doesn't matter how often it happens, every single time I laugh, and my eyes tickle with threatened tears, and I say, 'Hey baby. I see you.'

Clouds. Sunsets. Cardinals. Rainbows. Every single swirl in every single place—on coffee cups and waves on the beach and hairs on heads of babies and in art and at the movies and just every possible place. Each one filled my heart and lit up my soul. They still do. Every day.

Around the same time as I started noticing the signs, I also started noticing my thoughts during the day. I found myself in anger and frustration and denial more often than not. The words running through my mind, over and over were,

He should be here,
This is wrong,
He shouldn't have died,
I can't live without him,
This hurts so bad,
I can't fucking do this.

It was like a mantra of pain and disbelief.

Once I started seeing Rory signs everywhere, I realized that there might be another side to the fact that he left. Like, maybe it wasn't the most wrong thing that could ever happen.

Listen. This is a hard pill to swallow, and maybe it will get stuck. Maybe you will hate it. It took a long time for me to even look at it kindly. But maybe… maybe, if people are going to die—like, if we are all meant to die someday—that maybe death isn't the worst possible thing that can happen. Maybe the worst possible thing would be someone that we love and need and want not ever existing in the first place. Maybe, even though it hurts and feels awful, the fact that they lived is such a gift that it trumps everything else. Even their leaving.

Once I realized that, slowly, ever so slowly, I started replacing my mantra of pain with:

I was honored to birth him,

I was lucky to know him,
I was graced with his soul,
He didn't know a single day without love,
I can't wait to see him again.

It was a subtle shift. But over time… it made all the difference. Forever and ever, I am sad that he is gone. But more than that, so much more than that, I am grateful that he lived.

Grief in public is totally a bitch. Untenable. It feels absolutely impossible, and makes you want to avoid the public at all costs. The year that Rory was born, when I was under water and trying with desperation to find the surface, Brock and I started meeting for lunch on my therapy days. We'd meet at the restaurant next to Abbie's office, order our lunch, and then we'd sit outside and talk. It was a built-in weekly date, an hour of reconnecting without kids, and it was so lovely. I always looked forward to it.

We continued our weekly lunch dates after Rory died, only they were harder. Sadder. Quieter.

One afternoon, we had just finished eating and I didn't have the strength in me to walk back through the full restaurant of happy, glowing people to pay our bill. I asked Brock if he could please go do it, and I stayed where I was, sitting fully in the sun, allowing the radiant heat to warm my bones.

I sat there, quietly paying attention to my breath, and noticing the way the birds flitted around the trees next to me. I noticed the way the breeze played with my hair. I noticed the sounds of children shouting at a park just around the corner, and a smile touched the edges of my lips. I wondered if Rory was around. I wondered if he could see this perfect moment, sun-warmed and shiny, and filled with so many things to be grateful for above my sadness.

As I wondered, my awareness quietly turned towards the table next to mine, where another group had just been seated and it appeared that they were getting reacquainted. Two couples, each with a man and a woman, who were obviously meeting for lunch after an extended separation. They weren't talking loudly, nor was I particularly interested in their conversation, but something I couldn't put my finger on absolutely drew me in.

I don't even have distinct memories of each of them, just vague impressions. My eyes were closed for the entire conversation. I was so still and so peaceful that I didn't even shift as the tallest man sitting the farthest away from me almost immediately launched into a story of how he *had died* two weeks before. He had died. He told his table-mates that he was at the gym, and had apparently gone into a sudden cardiac arrest.

"I was on the treadmill," he said, "and then I was opening my eyes. There were medics around me, and everyone in the gym was standing and watching."

He didn't remember falling to the floor, nor the act of CPR being performed on his body. He didn't remember the defibrillator that restarted his heart, and he hardly remembered coming around a few minutes later.

"They told me I was gone for four minutes!" he related to his friends. I didn't see the tears that filled his eyes, but I heard them in his voice as he paused, and then went on thickly, "But all I can remember is just…peace. The most profound sense of incredible peace. It was so beautiful."

Sitting at the table next to them, with the sun shining fully on my face, tears poured silently down my cheeks as I thanked my sweet son yet again for sending me a message that he was okay. Where he was was beautiful. And all he felt was peace.

chapter 24

Deep grief began to soften its sharp corners into an ever-present, rounder sort of sadness. The empty space that Rory should have been in our lives was always glaringly obvious, but the stark pain wasn't quite so jagged. And as I looked forward to the years and years of my life I had left to live, I began to think about the possibility of the joy that another baby could bring—not to replace Rory; that could never be done. Rory was irreplaceable. I just couldn't help but imagine the joy that another baby could bring. Our baby had been taken from us, and having another was a big, scary, painful option. When I first brought it up to Brock, he immediately agreed with me—we should have another baby together.

Since he'd had the vasectomy relatively recently, we felt like it should be pretty easy to get it reversed. I started doing research into what it would look like and how much it would cost to get the procedure done. I found a surgeon with great statistics in the area, and the price-tag was steep — six thousand dollars for the whole thing, out of pocket. Insurance wasn't going to help cover that we'd changed our minds.

When Rory's death first went public, someone started a goFundme that raised close to twenty thousand dollars. That was a blessing, because it covered the very expensive cremation and urn, as well as the cost of the obituary, and both of the memorials. We didn't have to worry about those things, and it was kind. Lovely. Gentle. Loving. The money also covered what came to over ten thousand dollars in medical bills. Another absolute punch in the gut, to realize that even if your person dies, you still have to pay all of the bills. But again, we didn't have to cover it ourselves. That left just about six thousand dollars, almost exactly enough to cover the surgery and maybe a hotel stay, since the surgeon we had found was in a different city.

It seemed like the best possible way to spend the, "I'm so sorry your baby died" money. Up until we had decided to do the reversal, we had struggled with the money and what to do with it. Nothing felt quite right. Not spending it felt weird too. As soon as we had decided to reverse Brock's vasectomy, it was as though it was always meant to be. Peace and relief—that was what the money was meant for. And it would allow us to have another baby.

We, both of us, agreed that it made perfect sense, and scheduled the reversal, and paid the full fee up front.

I was so excited. I kept counting my blessings and hugging Brock spontaneously, immensely grateful that he was willing to go through with what seemed like a scary type of surgery, and that he wanted to have another baby with me. It was a glimmer of joy on the horizon. Something to look forward to. Another baby to birth, and snuggle, and cuddle, and love.

For weeks and weeks, I was counting down the days until the procedure. Brock seemed anxious, but all of our conversations were about what would happen after. How long it would take to heal, and when we could start fooling around again, and how long it might take to get pregnant. I even sent a text message to my midwife, asking if she would be willing to be with us through another birth.

Breathless excitement mingled with sorrow all the way up until exactly two weeks before the day of surgery when, out of the blue, Brock walked up to me in the kitchen and said, "I'm not doing it."

I shook my head as I tried to orient myself to him, to figure out what he was talking about. Not taking out the trash? Not making dinner?

"Not doing what?" I asked him, as I rinsed off dishes in the sink and put them into the dishwasher.

"The surgery. The vasectomy reversal thing. I'm not doing it. I cancelled it."

I stood there, frozen, hand hovering over the drawer in the dishwasher, water running forgotten in the sink. I blinked mutely as I looked directly into his eyes, and I tried to process what he had just told me.

"What… what do you mean you cancelled it?" Again, I shook my head, as though to shake away cobwebs. Surely he didn't mean what he just said. Surely not.

"I cancelled it. I got our money back. I'm not having the surgery, and I don't want to have another baby."

My eyes filled with tears before I even realized that I was hurting, and I demanded, "Why? Brock, why? Why not? What happened??"

He turned on his heel and shook his head no as he walked away from me, standing suddenly and starkly alone in front of the forgotten running water, unable to see or hear or comprehend what had just happened, or even have a glimmer understanding. I couldn't even wrap my mind around the idea that it was real.

No reversal.

No pregnancy.

No baby.

I was plunged back into the icy waters of grief, and it was more overwhelming than I could have imagined. I had already lost my Rory, and here, now, I was losing any possible potential future babies that we might have had. That glimmer of joy was snuffed out before it even had a chance to spark.

I was immediately desperate to talk him out of changing his mind. It was all I could think about, all I could talk about. I listened, I asked, I explained, I begged. I told him all of the great, wonderful, beautiful things about having another baby. I showed him pictures and videos of our other kids when they were small. I reminded him all of the things we loved about having our own baby; and don't get me wrong, Brock LOVES babies. He loves their little feet, and when they hold on to his finger, and they way they curl up into him. He loves the way they smile and laugh, and how excited they get when he comes home. He loves when they call him Dada, and he loves watching them change and learn and grow. A big man like him rarely gets to hold someone else's baby—generally, I think, dudes only get to hold their own, and he loves holding babies.

When asking and talking and begging and explaining didn't work, I moved on to threatening. Anger. Resentment. Frustration. *If you don't do this for me, I will never forgive you. I will always, always be angry at you.* He heard me, and didn't seem to care. It didn't shake him. He was immovable. Immutable. Implacable. He just wasn't going to do it.

I thought that losing Rory was the hardest thing that could ever happen to us, and if we survived that, our marriage must be indestructible. I had no idea how hard this new challenge was going to be to navigate. It very nearly tore us apart.

In the end, I realized that I couldn't force him to go through surgery to have another baby with me, and instead of fighting, I sought to understand.

When asked why he'd changed his mind, Brock would completely clam up. He couldn't talk about it openly, and seemed to draw in towards himself. Because I didn't understand, and desperately wanted to, I would continue poking and prodding, gently asking, probing. Brock would give weird, vague reasons—like *four kids is too many*, and *we don't have the money*, and *it's not fair to our other children.* All stuff that was realistically valid, but didn't really make sense in the grand scheme of things... because we'd already had four kids, we'd already afforded it, and it was wonderful. And our kids loved being four. Our living three, Ronan and Ruby and Ryder all wanted us to have another baby too.

It didn't happen quickly. We fought about it for weeks. I cried about it for months. There was no progress. No change. No give, no sudden insight, no closure. Just discomfort and pain that made no sense.

It was almost exactly a year later when Brock finally cracked open one night in bed as we cuddled, and told me what had shifted.

The day that Rory died, when Brock took him into the bedroom for a nap, he said that Rory was being wild and was overstimulated and overtired. He wouldn't lay down, and he wouldn't stop messing around, and Brock was getting irritated. Brock laid Rory back down over and over again, telling him it was time to go to sleep, and finally at peak frustration, he swatted Rory on his bottom.

"I spanked him, Mandy. The last thing I did before he died was spank him. I don't deserve to have another kid."

He broke down in sobs, and it was the first real, true thing I'd heard him say about having another baby since we said goodbye to our son. I immediately understood, and softened into deep compassion. I held him as he cried out that hard, dark shame. I felt some of that too; *why should I feel like I deserve another baby when we couldn't keep the one we had alive?* The one we loved and wanted and needed and failed.

As of the writing of this, eight years later, we still have not had another child. And likely won't. And while that feels big, sad, and hugely disappointing… It's also okay. I have never stopped wishing that Brock would change his mind, or that we would be gifted a miracle baby outside of the vasectomy reversal, and yet it has never come. I find some peace in allowing that, 'That's just how it's meant to be."

Not much, but a little.

chapter 25

Time passed, as time must, and eventually it was June. Four months from his death. Four months of hurting, healing, working, processing and trying to find joy and purpose again.

Rory was born in June, and the entrance to his birth month marked another milestone that took me by painful surprise. In that first year, each of the milestone days were so, so much worse than I could have imagined—and the dread leading up to them was nearly as bad. I didn't know what to do for Rory's birthday. He should have been turning two, and yet he never would be. I couldn't imagine doing nothing. There was nothing right to do.

But first I had to make it through my own birthday. I would turn 35 just seven days before Rory's birthday, and I didn't want to do it. I didn't want to celebrate another year of my life without him in it. I didn't want a party, and I didn't want cake, and I didn't want people to wish me a 'happy' birthday. "Happy" felt impossible. At the very, very best, I could manage a 'survived birthday'. One more day. One day closer to my boy.

It all felt so real, and so painful, and so massive while I was living in it, surrounded by it, crushed under the weight of it. Now, looking back, it feels so self-indulgent and petulant. It's hard to imagine something feeling that bad for that long, and yet I don't think I'm able to paint even a fraction of the picture of what it truly felt like; how deeply it destroyed me; how broken I was and thought I would forever be. Much like childbirth, and how we are able to forget! I know the pain was real. I believe it. But I've forgotten the true intensity of how the only wish that I could ever have for my birthday was to have my baby back, and it was never, ever going to happen, so I didn't want any of it. I gritted my teeth and held on through that day, doing nothing special at all, sitting on the couch and refusing to celebrate, and was glad to have it behind me.

Once I'd made it through my own birthday, I put my energy into Rory's, and pulled together a last minute party. I decided to make it an open invitation, and bring a ton of cakes—so many cakes—because Rory had never gotten to have cake. When he was alive, I was so strict and so controlling of everyone's diets that I didn't allow any sugar in our house. And my baby boy died without ever getting to taste the miracle of confection that is cake. So I bought cakes on cakes on cakes. Three full sized cakes (carrot, vanilla, and Oreo), and fifty cupcakes (assorted, and gluten free!). I didn't know how many people would show up, but I decided that there couldn't be too much cake. There was no such thing.

I also decided on boxes of smooth river rocks, and hundreds of paints, and bubbles for everyone, and we had a giant party in the park—with music, and games, and friends, and singing and laughter and joy. And when the whole group of something near 100 people that showed up sang "Happy Birthday" for Rory, I felt like we had done it. We had absolutely succeeded at celebrating him, honoring his life and remembering that he was here, he mattered, and he always would. He wouldn't be forgotten.

It felt like a tradition that we could continue forever.

Forever... or, until his next birthday. On Rory's next birthday, his third birthday, only something like 50 people showed up. I knew, rationally, that it was unrealistic for me to expect everyone to show up every year, over and over, for the rest of all time.

Irrationally, I didn't care. Emotionally, I was mad that they couldn't. Physically, it hurt. We had Rory's third birthday in the park, and it was beautiful, and I was just so absolutely grateful to everyone that came, while also carrying a hot pebble of sadness that it wasn't as big and magical as the year before, and it would never be that big and magical again.

As Rory's fourth birthday approached, I started to dread the idea of a birthday in the park. I knew that there would be even fewer friends there than from the year before, and it was heartbreaking for me. Understandable, but crushing. I wasn't sure that I could survive watching the numbers dwindle over and over until it was just us, all alone at the park, singing Happy Birthday to the sky with way too much cake.

The morning of Rory's fourth birthday, I curled up in bed and cried and cried. I didn't know what to do, and nothing felt right. I hadn't scheduled the Birthday in the Park. People were reaching out and asking what the plan was. I had no plan, was awash in grief and shame, and hated that everything felt so hard every single year.

Brock came into our bedroom with a cup of coffee he had fixed for me. He put the coffee down, and then crawled into bed beside me. He pulled me tightly into him, and let me cry.

"Where does it hurt?" he asked.

As soon as he said it, everything came pouring out. How awful it felt, and how I didn't know what to do, and that the birthday felt impossible, and everything, everything, everything was just wrong.

He squeezed me tightly, and asked, 'What do you think would help?' I shrugged and sniffled—there was nothing to be done. I didn't want to do anything but stay in bed all day and feel terrible.

Except, with a flash of inspiration, I suddenly imagined us, all of us, near the water, bathed in sunshine and windswept and smiling and covered in sand. I could feel the heat. I could smell the salt. It came to me as plain as I was there. I sat up suddenly, and exclaimed, "The beach!"

Brock looked at me with an eyebrow raised, his expression his question. "The beach!" I repeated. "Oh Brock, let's go to the beach for Rory's birthday." It felt so right as I was saying it, and I became more and more convinced that it was what we needed. What I needed. "Please oh please, please Brock… let's go to the beach."

Brock looked skeptical. It was going to be a long time in the car, and a lot to ask of a last minute trip. I started talking faster and faster, wiping away the dregs of the tears from before with the beginnings of a smile on my face. "We'll all just get into the car and drive to the beach and spend the day in the ocean and then come home," I was speaking so quickly I could hardly catch my breath, "It will absolutely be worth it and I think it's the only way that I'm going to survive today, and please oh please lets go to the beach."

"Okay, baby.' Brock smiled gently at me. 'Okay. Let's go to the beach."

I jumped out of bed like someone had lit a fire underneath me, and started shouting at the kids, 'Come on guys! We're going to the beach!'

It took us about 30 minutes to gather bathing suits and towels and a few snacks for the road, and without hesitating or second guessing, we were in the car and headed for Folly Beach. The drive was 3.5 hours, and it was well after noon when we got there. We parked on the street and unloaded our meager supplies, and ran down to the water… and it was miraculous.

The wind, the water, the waves, and the smiles on everyone's faces. I breathed the ocean air in so deeply, and looked around at my family, and the other beach-goers, and the sea, and I knew. It was absolutely the right choice. My heart was so full, and my whole family was so happy, and the ocean was just so healing. We were at the water, and it was magic. There was a sadness that Rory wasn't there to enjoy it with us… but also, he kinda sorta was.

We stayed until everyone started to get tired, and then dressed back up in our dry clothes and walked to a nearby restaurant. We ate dinner on the roof and watched the sun start to sink behind the buildings. Every single one of us was red-faced, filled up with joy and adventure, and even though it was going to be a long ride home, it was just so worth it.

We drove home in the dark and didn't get everyone in bed until nearly midnight. Rory's birthday was over, and it was a perfect,

perfect day. I knew that we had come up with something that could be a tradition that we could usher forward for forever. And we have. And we will. On June 29th, you will find us at the beach.

I was starting to get a handle on it.

Can you get a handle on grief?

There is this prevailing belief that there is 'no wrong way to grieve,' but I don't agree with that. I really don't.

There is absolutely a wrong way to grieve, and that is to *not do it*.

I think a whole lot of people who have lost someone spend a whole lot of time <u>not</u> grieving. And I don't blame them. It's exhausting. And sad. And it hurts. No one wants to do it. It's so much easier to avoid it—until it's not.

The thing is, I think the deeply painful part of grief is finite—it doesn't last forever. There is some unit, some amount, some value of grief that you must go through, and feel all of it in order to come out the other side.

I don't know how much it is, or how to quantify it, but I know that it ends.

And, I don't think that you have to do it all at once. As a matter of fact, I don't think it's possible to do it all at once. But it's possible to do as much of it as you can handle at a time. Maybe a day. Maybe an hour. Maybe only a few moments—where you just let yourself feel it all. The hugeness of it. The hurt of it. The universal wrongness of the fact that the person that you loved so very much is gone. You feel it all, and you let it hurt, and you let it pour all the way out of you.

You do this thing, over and over, whenever you can, whenever it is possible… and then, at some point, you come out the other side. Where you can ease yourself into a softer grief, into grieving, the kind that *does* last forever, and it doesn't hurt quite so much. Maybe it's because you've gone through the minefield of the agony of the first grief, the loss, or maybe it's because you've gotten better at it. I don't know. What I know is that you *have to do it*.

Not doing it? That looks like numbing. Doing anything possible to not feel all of the things. There are so, so many ways to numb, and some of them are *so necessary*—so we can function on a daily basis. But if numbing continues over and over, again and again, in order to not feel... Well, those become addictions. And those CAN kill you. And all of that emotion and feeling and turmoil and pain that you have from the loss, that entire chunk or helping or amount of whatever it is that you have to go through — it stays trapped inside of you, and weighs you down.

As I was stewarding my grief, I came to realize it felt like it was gathering up in a bucket. All of the grief feelings that I had or felt or collected would build up inside of me like I was hefting it around. It came with me everywhere. And it was weighty. The only way to get it out, to empty the burden of it, to put it down, was to do what I started to call 'tipping my bucket'.

Tipping the bucket meant I had to *feel the grief*. To let it out of me. To talk or cry or wail or sob. To ache. To hurt *all the way*. I had to tip the bucket in order to lighten the load and feel okay again. I noticed that the longer I went without tipping my grief out, the harder it was to tip—just like a real bucket. As it got too full, it got heavier and heavier, and harder to tip over.

Harder to tip meant harder to start the grief moving again. Like I was hardening up and becoming numb. Like I knew it was going to hurt so much when I got it flowing, so I started avoiding it more and more. And the longer I avoided it, the harder it was to start the bucket tipping!

As soon as I noticed this—that the start of the tipping was harder, and the release more painful—I started finding ways to intentionally tip myself into grief. I wanted to empty my bucket more often, in smaller amounts. I decided that I didn't want to let my bucket get full. I didn't want to carry all that weight around, and I didn't want the burden of a giant, painful release.

I began tipping my bucket out every single day, and I figured out what things would get the grief flowing. Music was always an easy place to go to get the tears to start. There were songs that reminded me so much of Rory that just hearing the first notes would immediately make me cry. Pictures were another safe place to begin a tipping. Videos. Scrolling instagram and reading the captions of moments in his life. If Brock was tipping his bucket out, I would sit with him, and mine would tip out alongside his. Talking to Brock about how I was feeling—being honest and saying the hard things—always helped. "I'm in grief today, baby." That was all it took. I never had to defend myself or explain myself. It was always just okay. He met me there, and sat with me, in grief, for as long as I needed—and I did the same for him.

As we moved forward, we realized there were other choices that we could make that helped us to live. They were choices that were a little harder, but make no mistake, they were still choices.

We had the choice to let go of the anger—of the righteousness and wrongness and betrayal of life. We had the choice to stop being so mad at the world and at the universe and at existence for letting it happen, for letting our baby die. We had the choice to unclench our jaws, and relax our shoulders down away from our ears. We could choose to let the tension go from our bodies. I was angry that it was a choice. I didn't want to get to choose those things. It felt good to be angry at the world for being just so fucked up that someone could lose a child, and that someone could be me. But the anger was a poison in my soul, and I didn't want to carry that around either.

So we eventually realized that we must forgive. We could choose to forgive. We decided that we MUST choose to forgive.

To forgive Rory for dying.

To forgive ourselves for not being able to stop it.

To forgive life for being life.

To forgive death for being death.

With that choice, with that forgiveness came a softening, an opening, an acceptance. It was not what we wanted, nor was it anything we would ever have chosen—but it *was*. And because it was, we chose to let go of the anger, and the guilt, and the shame, and instead found that space to forgive.

I don't believe that Rory is sad that he died before me. I definitely don't believe he wants me here spending the rest of my time on this planet mired in deep and painful guilt because he died before I did, and that I am still living. I choose to believe that, if he gets to wish for anything, it is to see his family feeling free, joyful, expansive, and happy to be alive. I never, ever want to forget that *life* is the gift. Death is a certainty—living is the miracle. We are here. We get to be here.

For months and months after Rory died, I constantly thought the words, *My baby died, and I have to keep living.*

Eventually, there was a shift, when I realized that I had thought to myself that day, *My baby died, and I get to keep living.*

chapter 26

Months and months passed. Rory was still dead, and yet life stubbornly continued. My kids were in school, and I was getting a handle on functioning again, and it seemed like it was finally time to look forward instead of back.

Before Rory died, I had allowed myself to dream of becoming a midwife.

And then, he was gone and I didn't know what I wanted. I didn't know what I could do, or what I would be capable of, or what would hurt too much to look at. Since I didn't know who I was, I didn't know if I still had the same dream.

I thought that helping women through birth could be massively healing for me. But I also knew that birth is one of the last true bastions of life and death, impossibly close to the veil, and a huge, hard, powerful responsibility. I didn't know that I could do it. I didn't know if I was enough.

My homebirth midwife, Stephanie, was still out there, somewhere. Before Rory died, I had stated my desire and intention to become an assistant, to start a traditional apprenticeship in midwifery. Her original response was vague and unpromising. I was anxious about reaching out again. I didn't really know how long an apprenticeship would take, I didn't really know if I was a good candidate, and I didn't know if she would ever pick me.

Then, one morning in October, eight months after Rory's death, Stephanie texted me out of the blue that her usual assistant was sick, and asked if I wanted to come help out in prenatals. I had already dropped the older kids at school, but Ryder was in the car with me. I texted back my reply, a resounding "YES!" before I had even begun to think about childcare. I told her I would be a little late, but I was on my way.

I called Brock and asked him to please work from home that day. He was so excited for me, and was willing to help out in any way that he could to make it happen. I dropped Ryder off at home, and had my neighbor to stay with him for the 20 minutes it would take for Brock to get home, and then I headed to my first day of prenatals.

I was hooked. Immediately. That day, in that room, holding space for and spending time with those pregnant women—for the first time since Rory died, I felt like I had something outside of myself and my family to focus on, some greater purpose, and it was magnificent. I came home on cloud nine, exhausted but enchanted, totally drained but completely filled up, and I was powerfully driven to *keep going*.

I received another invitation to prenatals the following week, and one of the ladies that showed up that day was Nancy and her husband, Tomis. She was almost a week past her 'guess date', and Steph had her come to her prenatal visit to get her out of her house. During her visit, I noticed that she seemed to be having contractions every 10 or 15 minutes or so. She looked beautiful and healthy at her appointment, and all of her vitals checked out. Her baby sounded glorious, and it occurred to me that she might be in early labor. Stephanie recommended that she and her husband go out for lunch somewhere, and not head home until labor had advanced enough that she couldn't *possibly* stay out any longer. Nancy left, and I was thrilled for them.

At the end of the day, tired but full, Steph stopped me as I was walking out to my car to head home. "I think Nancy is in labor. Would you like to join me at this birth?"

I don't know that I have ever been so excited. I definitely had not felt that level of elation since Rory died. It was Hallowe'en, and I was supposed to take my kids trick or treating. Going to that birth meant missing the holiday. Saying yes to a possible life meant saying no to my family. It meant choosing midwifery over a memory. I knew in that moment that I was going to have to choose midwifery over my family again and again and again. It was a lot to ask of my husband and my kids who had already lost so much.

I got in my car, texted Brock that I was going to a birth(!!!) and that I didn't know when I'd be home. He was immediately ecstatic for me, and promised to take a ton of pictures. He gave me zero guilt and nothing but support. Then I followed Steph's car to Nancy's home, and my life was forever changed.

When we arrived, I was filled with nerves, a bundle of anxious energy. Nancy was in a birth pool, with soft meditation type music playing in the background. She was breathing deeply and moaning gently through her contractions. I had been to so few births that I really had no idea what was happening, except the work of labor. It was her first baby, and I had no frame of reference for how long we would be there, or what it could look like.

Stephanie set up all of her birth equipment, and then we just settled in. To be 'with woman.' To hold space. To watch a powerful human do a powerful thing, and simply believing that she could.

We were in the kitchen of a small apartment at the top of a home-based school building; a child-led haven of nature and safety on a wooded acre lot in the middle of down-town Charlotte. The sun was setting, and there were no lights on. We could hear cars driving by distantly underneath the sounds of birds calling right out the window. It was close in the room; hot and humid, with no AC running in a warm Southern October, and Nancy's face was lit with the soft glow of the golden hour on her sweat soaked forehead.

It became clear, to even my inexperienced eye, that Nancy was getting closer and closer to birthing her baby as she started gently pushing at the top of contractions. I'm not even entirely sure she knew she was pushing. She was on another planet.

This is the strongest, most beautiful woman alive, I thought as she pushed through another contraction.

Stephanie had moved closer to the birthing tub to watch as Nancy began to deliver her baby. She was in a deep goddess squat in the water, holding on to either side, and roaring through her powerful pushes. No one was telling her what to do. No one touched her. Stephanie, her husband, her doula and I—we all just witnessed her power in awe and admiration.

I quietly edged closer to the pool, trying to see what Stephanie was doing as the baby was born into the water. But just as she completed her final push, Nancy suddenly allowed her weight to fall backwards, and the baby came forwards between her legs instead of behind her. "I don't have the baby," I heard Stephanie's voice from behind. Without thinking, I replied, "I've got him," and reached out my hands and handed the baby up to Nancy's waiting arms as she sat down in the tub, and leaned back in relief.

Completion. Ecstasy.

The baby looked utterly perfect, crying and breathing and doing all of the right things. I backed away as Stephanie handed me a towel to dry my arms, and we just stood there and witnessed as Nancy and Tomis became a family with their brand new son.

I was in awe. My body shook, and shook, and shook. The adrenaline, the oxytocin, the cortisol—all of my body's most potent hormones were pumping furiously through my veins. It was otherworldly.

And, after a few moments that felt like eternity, Stephanie leaned over and quietly said, 'Maybe some towels?'

Her gentle direction shook me out of my reverie and gave me purpose again. *Towels*!

A peaceful immediate post-birth saw us leaving Nancy's home to the dim light of a cloudless sky full of stars. I gazed up in wonder as I walked to my car. I was so. Fucking. Full.

Of life. Of Joy. Of Wonder. Of passion. I knew it. I knew who I was. In that moment, I knew that I was going to be a midwife. Birth was my calling, and the voice was loud and clear and real and true.

A few weeks later, Stephanie and I were having lunch together, and she asked me if I thought that I was truly ready to start attending births regularly. I was a little confused and asked her what she meant by 'ready'.

"Well," she paused, "... sometimes, at a birth, when things don't go well, or the baby has a tough time, we have to *resuscitate*. We have to help that baby to breathe. That's part of the job, you know—to help the baby to breathe. And you have to be able to do it. You can't freak out, or pause, or freeze—you just have to do the job." She was kind. Soft. Open. I understood that she needed to be sure. "Do you think you're ready?"

I stayed silent and considered for a few long moments. *Was I ready?* Is that something that exists? Is it possible to know you are ready for something before that thing occurs? Or is readiness just a wishful thought that we have when facing something unknown, and only ever found in retrospect?

"I think," I said slowly, "I think, honestly, that my ability to do CPR on my own baby when it was required feels solidly like proof to me that I will be able to do what needs to be done in the moment." I paused a moment, caught my breath, and continued, "And this might sound heartless... but doing CPR on someone else's baby will never, ever be harder than doing it on my own."

I looked up and met her eyes and said with complete confidence, "Steph, I honestly don't think I'll have a problem with it."

Stephanie believed me, and started inviting me to births with her regularly. Over the next several weeks I attended and assisted at her next ten births—all ten of which delivered a baby that required a resuscitation. I did not cry. Ten babies that needed help to breathe at birth, I did not cry. Ten scenarios where I stood in a room and watched Stephanie help an infant to start breathing, mouth to mouth, reminiscent of the moments I had wished that my own baby would live—I did not cry. I was so totally brand new to birth work that I didn't have to provide any of the life saving skills, but I did have to watch them. And I did not cry.

After the tenth encounter with a baby that took more than a normal amount of resuscitation to come around and start breathing on her own, Steph stopped me outside after the birth and put her hands on my shoulders.

"I need you to know right now," she told me firmly, "That this is *not* a normal amount of resuscitation. I don't think I've ever had this many in a row before. And I don't think it's an accident. I think you are being asked if you can really, really handle this. The universe is asking you, 'are you sure?'."

She hugged me tightly, and said that she was thankful for me, and glad that I was there.

On my way home, I asked myself again, *am I sure?*

Do I really want this?

It was big and huge and awful, sometimes. Babies didn't breathe right away sometimes. Mamas had issues with bleeding sometimes. And all of that was really scary. I tried to quiet my thoughts and focus on my breathing, and what kept coming up for me in my mind was, "*Why? Why? Why am I doing this?*" After a while, I realized that I needed to get clear on my WHY.

Why did I want to be a midwife? What was the reason I was even willing to start on that journey?

I knew it without any hesitation or doubt. I wanted to be a midwife because more women needed access to the kind of care I had during my own home births. My *why* was that I believed so powerfully that there needed to be more midwives… and I could do that.

I could do it.

I knew that, so long as my *why* was bigger than my fear, I was going to be okay. With my why in my heart, I was sure.

At the next birth, after a sweet, short, powerful labor, a baby was pushed out into the world and breathed without assistance—cried out with power and purpose and pleasure, "*I am born!*"

And, upon seeing a baby be born that *did not* need any kind of resuscitation, I finally broke down and cried, and cried, and cried.

chapter 27

Our first Christmas without Rory rolled around. Ten months gone. I knew it was going to be painful, but I drastically underestimated how hard the holidays would be. I wanted to curl up in bed and hibernate until January. I didn't want to do any of it. I was just so tired of feeling all of the pain. Grief came and went so wildly, and it *was* hard and heavy. It couldn't be any other way.

Despite the pain, Brock and I knew that we didn't want our sweet living three to feel like all of the joy in the world ended with the loss of their baby brother. So, through the ache and tears, we did all of the Christmas things without our Rory, and just let it hurt.

We set up the Christmas tree, and I wished that he could be there to see it. We unpacked the decorations and played Christmas music while the kids put the bulbs and garland on the tree. My view blurred beautifully as I imagined Rory wandering in and out around the boxes of Christmas things, and how excited he would be. I missed the boughs at toddler height, overloaded with all of the colors on the same branch the way babies do. I missed having the glass ornaments up high where he wouldn't reach them. I missed hearing his little voice as he learned the carols we shared every year.

We baked cookies and I missed his little grubby hands grabbing at the chocolate chips, and the way his eyes would have lit up at a taste of raw cookie dough. I missed getting to see him squatting in front of the oven in anticipation of warm chocolate chip cookies and a glass of milk. I missed getting to see his growing sense of excitement and understanding about the packages under the tree, and knowing that Christmas morning without him was just going to feel impossible.

And then it was Christmas Eve, and all of the things were done. The presents were wrapped, and the stockings were filled, and there was a plate of cookies next to the fire. Brock and I were sitting on the couch together, sipping on hot cocoa. I was feeling a deep contentment in my soul, I thought to myself, "We did it. I don't know how we did it, and it was hard as hell, but we survived the year without Rory," and the sense of accomplishment bloomed within me.

We did it. It is over.

And in that self-same moment, I realized that I *was* still waiting for it to all be over. Like Rory dying was a bad dream that I was going to wake up from. Like all we had to do was just survive the year without Rory, and *it would all be over.* Like if I just handled it with beauty and compassion and strength and grace, he would come back. Like none of it was real. In that instant, I recognized that I was *still* just waiting for him to come back. It still wasn't real yet. I truly hadn't accepted it.

Oh God.

He was really gone.

He wasn't ever coming back.

Even though we had survived the year.

Even though we had made it, and hadn't let grief wreck us.

Even though it was Christmas, and we were okay.

Even though we were happy sometimes.

He was really gone, and he was never coming back.

I broke down into the big, heavy, empty, sobbing grief cry, right there on the couch next to Brock where I had just been basking in the warm glow of contentment and joy.

It shook me to the depths of my soul.

Rory is never, ever coming back.

It wasn't just that, though. It wasn't just that I kept waiting for him to come back. That it hadn't truly sunk in that he was gone forever.

I also realized that I had been celebrating in my mind that *we did it* meant that we *never had to do it again*. That we survived death and grief and turmoil and heartbreak. We lost our son, and that was it. We were done. Finished. We passed! Game over.

Guys. We weren't done. That deep aching moment of grief was also a moment of earth-shaking realization: Rory was not the last person we loved to die, *Rory was the first*.

It wasn't the last time we would have to go through and feel all of that pain, it was the first time.

From that moment forward, for the rest of our lives, there was always going to be the possibility and the reality that other people we love are going to die, and they will break me open and wreck me just as much. My parents, Brock's parents, our siblings, our friends, our other children and each other. All of those losses were still yet to come.

Rory was not the last, he was the first.

A few short weeks later, we were approaching the actual anniversary of Rory's death. One full rotation around the sun since he died. The physical date and time, the milestone of him leaving. Walking towards that day was almost as hard as losing him in the first place. Looking back at pictures from before he died, those beautiful people had no idea what was coming, nor what they were about to endure. It broke my heart for them; for me; for us.

I was immensely frustrated rolling into February. I was hurt by the fact that there was no word in the English language to describe the anniversary of dying. Even that—anniversary of death—sounded so wrong. I didn't particularly love the oft-used, "angel-versary" either. Death day? Gross. There had to be something to call the day that Rory died that didn't feel quite so cumbersome and awful.

At some point, on Instagram, I had started to refer to Rory as my "sweet-baby-gone" rather than 'my dead child' or 'my baby that died.' It was more right. And somehow, just as naturally as swirls became the symbol of his presence, and bubbles made me feel like he was around, the anniversary of his death became Rory's "gone-day." Even that isn't perfect, because he is still here—he's still around, and watching and loving and caring for us. I know he's not really gone… just different. But gone-day gave me the right feelings, and sounded the right way, and it stuck.

Rory's first gone-day came and went, and it was just as hard as I had expected it to be. The fact is, you don't just lose your child one time—you lose them over and over and over again. We hunkered down in the house, and burned candles, and spoke to him, and promised him over and over and over that we would never forget him, that he would always matter to us, and we'd never let his memory fade. And I cried, and cried and cried.

His next gone-day, we decided to be in the woods. We went for a hike, and the big kids complained and whined and crabbed about the weather, and the rain, and the cold, and how they just wanted to go home. It reminded me that the kids really just didn't care about what was going on for us, physically or emotionally, and it was really hard not to take it personally. So we got hot cocoa on the way home, and Brock and I promised ourselves that we would never take our kiddos on a memorial gone-day outing again.

Rory's third gone-day, we didn't tell the kids. We did absolutely nothing special. We didn't go out, we didn't hike, and we didn't make it memorable in any way at all. The weather was awful, and I started to feel like every year was a reflection of the cold, steely, awful murky day that he fell into the lake and left us. Ruby and Ryder, unknowingly both had terrible, awful, emotionally hard days, and when we told them that it was the anniversary of the day Rory died, we realized that it didn't make sense to not tell them—they were feeling it in their bodies, too.

On Rory's fourth gone-day, we got a puppy. I know. I know. But it seemed like the right idea at the time. I also went back to my tattoo artist, and had her forever-ink a portrait of my boy on my shoulder, and she did. It was (and is) perfect.

Rory's fifth gone-day, Brock and I let the kids stay home from school, and then we went to a horse ranch and did a session of equine therapy. It was beautiful, and peaceful, and brilliant, and lovely... and exactly right.

I don't know what we'll do next year.

chapter 28

It has been seven fucking years since Rory died. We have survived seven gone days and seven Christmases, and seven years of birthdays without him. I can't believe we have survived. It has been awful.

It has been wonderful.

One of the hardest parts of coming back to life is realizing that you are not sad all the time. You aren't broken all the time. You aren't mournful and dismal and depressed all the time.

That allowing comes with its own pain. It's bittersweet, because it is actually quite wonderful to keep living, and to see brilliant, beautiful, breathtaking magic everywhere you look. But it also feels like a betrayal. Like, by being okay, and by being gloriously happy, you are leaving them behind. You are "ok" that they died. That maybe you don't miss them anymore, or somehow being happy means you love them less. It is a beautiful, painful contradiction, because it gets to be both.

We are coming up on Rory's 8th gone-day, and life has continued. Sometimes painfully, sometimes so wonderfully that it hurts. Through it all, I have nothing but gratitude—for my beautiful life, my gorgeous kids, my doting husband, and a career that has given me back my passion and my dreams.

I am now a fully certified Midwife in my own right, taking care of my own clients and making a difference in the world for birthing mamas the way the difference has been made for me. It's really for real—that all of my wildest dreams have come true. I have everything I'd ever dreamed of, and more.

Recently, we had a birth that went sideways before it even started. The mama was having her fourth baby, and we had helped her with her third. She was strong and healthy and beautiful—and had incredible, fast, easy births. This time, there was some blood in her amniotic fluid when her water broke, which is not, strictly-speaking, normal. We arrived and listened to the baby, and the baby's heart rate sounded lower than we expected—it was clear that we needed to immediately rush to the hospital. She was taken back for a crash emergency surgery, and it was still too late. Mama was okay, but the baby did not survive. For some unknown reason, and with no risk factors, her placenta had completely separated from her mother, and she died before she was born.

Stephanie and I stayed in the car in the hospital parking lot all night, waiting to see and support the mother and father in their deepest, darkest loss. There was no other thing to do—it was the only right thing.

When we went up to see them in the morning, the mother was holding her sweet, perfect still baby. She, the baby, was just so beautiful. She looked healthy and immaculate and exquisite... and not alive. It made no sense. It couldn't make sense. We stood with the mother as she poured out her grief and disbelief. I knew exactly how she felt. Her sweet daughter was gone. And it was utterly unfair.

The hospital had dressed the baby in a satin *angel gown* covered in sequins and beads. It was nice, on some level, to have the baby dressed in something. But... it wasn't hers. I told the mother that I had brought some clothes from their home—some of her clothes set aside for her baby girl. I asked her if she wanted to put them on her daughter. The mother nodded, and held up her arms, full of IVs and bracelets and showing that her hands were swollen. "I don't think I can do it," she explained. She asked me if I would be willing to dress the baby. I told her, with tears in my eyes, that it would absolutely be my greatest honor.

And it was. I undressed her baby from the strange silken, saccharine angel gown that the hospital had dressed her in, and lovingly put her into clothes that were hers, meant for her, set aside specifically for her. I whispered quietly and lovingly to her—I told her I was so sorry she couldn't stay. I remembered the man with the wire rimmed glasses as I gently picked up the beautiful girl child, and wrapped her in a floral blanket. It was holy. It may have been the holiest thing I had ever done.

I held the baby for a moment, and then asked her father, "Will you please hold your baby?" I knew he hadn't yet, and maybe he didn't want to. I remembered how it felt to not want to hold my own baby after he had died. But I also knew how angry I was at myself for just leaving him at the hospital, for not having the space to hold him and care for him after he was gone. I wish someone had told me to. I knew how bad that regret felt, so I asked him to hold his daughter.

As he received his baby girl, he broke into sobs—and I was so glad he said yes. Dads get overlooked. We took pictures for them, because the pictures matter so much. We talked to them about their options, because mostly the hospital doesn't. And then we gave all of our love and said goodbye, and left them. There wasn't any more we could do.

That day, I felt like I had finally paid forward all of the love and care and tenderness that was shown to me when my own baby died, a ripple in the pool of life. I could see the rings moving outward, farther and farther from the center—and felt that we are so much more connected than we think we are.

We stood together in the parking lot outside of the hospital, Steph and I, ready to part ways.

"That was rough," I said, eyes rimmed with redness and filled with tears that hadn't fallen yet.

"It was, friend." She looked at me unwaveringly, piercingly, straight in the eye, and right into my soul. "But that's the job," she continued. "Being a midwife means being 'with women,' regardless of what comes. The good and the bad. The hard and the magnificent.

The light and the dark. That's why we are here."

And of course, she was right. That's the job.

I think, possibly, it's not just the job of midwives — it is the job of life. To stick with it, to stick with each other, regardless of what comes.

Today, it's me. Tomorrow, it might be you. It is always someone. And we can all get through it, all of us—we can come out on the other side—as long as we do it *together.*

afterword

nd one final note about the darkness: it has never fully disappeared from my life. It comes and goes—ebbs and flows—just like joy and grief. What I've finally come to understand is that the darkness was never the enemy. The goal was never to banish it completely. The goal was to learn how to sit with it. To let it be.

And while I've never exactly welcomed the darkness, I've come to know—deeply—that its presence matters. The gloom, the blackness, the inky murk… without it, I wouldn't know how to orient myself.

Now, I've learned to let the darkness fall behind me. And when it does, I can turn—wholly and fully and resolutely—towards the light.

acknowledgments

I think writing a book is one part desire, and ten parts support. This book absolutely wouldn't have happened without the encouragement and faith from a multitude of folks that cheered me on in a multitude of ways.

First, Adrienne Schenck—who believed that a book was possible long before anyone else, and stuck with me through to the bitter end. Becca Grischow—book coach extraordinare, who took a word-vomit half-book and helped form it into an actual manuscript, all while supporting my delicate self-esteem. *No Ruth!* My beta readers: Bri Hurlburt, Becky Kiser, Mom, Laura McCorry... I think it's possible that there were other beta readers, but I had a stroke between now and then, and memory is no longer one of my strong suits. Please forgive me. I'd like to thanks Elize Vas for giving me a final edit and championing me so loudly. And Jasmine Hromjak—for creating a cover that felt like mine, the interior formatting, and mainly just being wonderful.

I want to thank all of the families that allowed me to share their names and stories inside of my own—walking through your experiences shaped me deeply. Also, while many of the names in this book have been changed, the people who showed up in the real story—I am still thankful. For all of it. Even the parts that ended. Stephanie Snow - the deepest and longest and truest of thanks. You show up over and over in so many ways.

Thank you to my children. Thank you for choosing me. Thank you for loving me. Thank you - I love you - I'm sorry - Please forgive me.

And of course, I must also thank my partner and husband, Brock. My hero, my sidekick, my true North. It was rough there, for a while. But we don't get to be *here* without having been there first. I'm so glad we made our way through it all—together.

about the author

M andy Allender is a Canadian born woman living in the Carolinas. She has been a lifelong reader and writer, sharing her thoughts online since 2004. She spends her time on her 14-acre farm with her husband, Brock, and three living children, Ronan, Ruby, and Ryder. She loves books, fiber crafts, and sitting by the fire. She hates small talk, the question "What's for dinner?," and laundry. She can be found on TikTok and Instagram, both @Tempestbeauty (the name she came up with when she joined AOL instant messenger at 14) and would love to connect. *Of Water and Grief* is the product of an overwhelming love of storytelling, a deep-seated willingness to be vulnerable, and a powerful need to share the voice of sorrow. Mandy continues to attend births with her partner, Stephanie, and loves every second of it.

www.ingramcontent.com/pod-product-compliance
Lightning Source LLC
Chambersburg PA
CBHW031508120626
46545CB00005B/1788